Also by Mark C. Bodanza

A Game That Forged Rivals
*How Competition Between Two New England High Schools
Created One of the Greatest Traditions in Football*

1933
Football at the Depth of the Great Depression

Make It Count
The Life and Times of Basketball Great JoJo White

Resolve and Rescue
*The True Story of Frances Drake and the
Anti-Slavery Movement*

Ten Times a Champion
The Story of Basketball Legend Sam Jones

Leominster Chronicles
Tales from the Comb City

Rivals
More About the Fitchburg-Leominster Football Tradition

Risk Takers & History Makers
The Story of Leominster

His first children's book: ***She Took a Stand***
The Story of Frances Drake and the Underground Railroad

Hostage Terror
Ralf Traugott and the Hijacking of Flight 847

When the Lion Roared
How Lou Little Helped Shape College Football

Johnny Appleseed
The Man Behind the Folklore

Enlightenment & Enchantment

Two Men Who Shaped American Culture

NORTH HILL PRESS
Leominster, Massachusetts
2025

Copyright © 2025 by Mark C. Bodanza

All rights reserved

No part of this book may be reproduced, stored or transmitted in any form or by any means, electronic or mechanical, including photocopying, recording or by any information storage and retrieval system, without the written permission of the publisher, except in case of brief quotation embodied in critical articles and reviews.

This book is not authorized, sponsored, or endorsed by the Walt Disney Company or any of its subsidiaries. It is an unofficial and unauthorized book and not a Disney product. Mentions of names and places associated with Disney and its affiliated businesses are not intended in any way to infringe on any existing copyrights or registered trademarks of the Walt Disney Company but are used in context for educational and journalistic purposes.

Illustrated by Steve Legere
Book and cover design by Robin Wrighton

ISBN: 978-0-9970144-9-5
Library of Congress Control Number: 2024918140

Bodanza, Mark C.
Enlightenment & Enchantment
Two Men Who Shaped American Culture

Published by

NORTH HILL PRESS

36 School Street
Leominster, MA 01453

Northhillpress.com

For information on publishing with North Hill Press,
or for special purchases contact: info@northhillpress.com

Printed in Lowell, Massachusetts by King Printing Co., Inc.

"[w]hen I argue that Mickey Mouse may in fact be more important to an understanding of the 1930s than Franklin Roosevelt, audiences snicker. The shaping of government remains a significant thing, ...[b]ut if we want to know how people experienced the world, FDR had his role but so did Mickey Mouse."

Walter Susman 1984,
renowned cultural historian,
Rutgers University

Dedication

To my wife Adele, children Melissa, Kathryn and Nicholas, son-in-law Dalton and grandchildren Brody and Adelina too, thank you for always being there, for understanding and most of all for your unending love and support.

Contents

Introduction xiii

Chapter 1: The Conversion of Benjamin
Franklin Begins 1

Chapter 2: The Letter Affair 13

Chapter 3: Walt Disney Discovers Television 21

Chapter 4: Walt Disney's Formative Years 29

Chapter 5: Of Indenture and Escape 37

Chapter 6: The Early Trials and Tribulations
of Franklin and Disney 43

Chapter 7: Franklin Takes a Wife 53

Chapter 8: Walt Goes West 63

Chapter 9: Success Visits Again 73

Chapter 10: Electricity Propels Franklin's Stature 79

Chapter 11: Disney's Restless Mind Looks Ahead 87

Chapter 12: Franklin Pursues a New Vocation 95

Chapter 13: Walt Disney Reinvents the
American Vacation 103

Chapter 14: Franklin Takes a Role on a
Larger Stage 115

Chapter 15: Walt Changes the Entertainment
World 125

Chapter 16: Guiding the Ship of State 133

Chapter 17: Taking His Show East 141

Chapter 18: Making Peace 151

Chapter 19: Walt's Last Dream 159

Chapter 20: Building a Nation 167

Epilogue 179
Endnotes 195

Introduction

They were born 195 years apart and into very different worlds, Benjamin Franklin on January 17, 1706, in Boston, Massachusetts, and Walt Disney on December 5, 1901, in Chicago, Illinois. Each had multiple siblings, though Franklin's family was more than triple the size of Disney's. Franklin had sixteen brothers and sisters, ten from his father's first marriage. Once their mother died and Josiah Franklin remarried, seven more children, including Benjamin Franklin, followed. Disney had three brothers and a sister. Franklin had only two younger siblings and Disney just one, but each was the youngest son of their family.

Despite the separation of nearly two centuries, it would be hard to imagine two people who have had a greater impact on the American psyche. Their contributions to our culture are innumerable. Keen observers, their ability to understand us, the inhabitants of this swath of North America, helped shape who we are in ways that have few parallels.

The timeline of the American experience is filled with many notables, scientists, architects of statecraft, leaders, entertainers, and titans of business. While those doers and risk-takers are an important part of our fabric, few have had the pervasive and lasting impact of Franklin and Disney.

Abraham Lincoln and Franklin Roosevelt led us through wars that threatened the American republic and world order. Madison, Jefferson, Adams, and Hamilton helped create the organs of American government. Morse,

Bell, and Edison advanced the cause of communication and Fulton, Ford, and the Wright brothers propelled transportation in significant ways. There are scores of other American inventors who helped change the world we live in, including Eli Whitney, George Washington Carver, Charles Goodyear, Nikola Tesla, Jonas Salk, Robert Goddard and Steve Jobs to name just a few. Many changed the society they lived in. Few could argue the impact of Frederica Douglass, Harriet Tubman, Susan B. Anthony, Elizabeth Cady Stanton, Henry David Thoreau, or Jackie Robinson. And then there were those who entertained us. Washington Irving, Mark Twain, Louis Armstrong, Elvis Presley, and Jimmy Hendrix are worthy of mention among a group in the hundreds.

Their claims to significance are great but Benjamin Franklin stands alone. Many have said that Franklin was the first American. He was not the first to the cause of revolution, but the case is strong that without him the revolution would have never gotten off the ground. The American colonists were keenly aware of the stakes as well as the penalty for treason. The debate over American independence was spirited and the issue far from decided for a time. There were voices who sought reconciliation, or at least a more tempered approach. Not until Franklin came over to the cause of independence was the matter decided.

Franklin was the one American colonist who carried the pedigree of a gentleman, a man of preeminence and of unquestioned stature. He valued his place in a world that included the British Empire. He was loath to separate from a mother country that was in many ways the source of his credentials. The story of how Franklin was finally persuaded to plant two feet firmly on the side of

Introduction

American independence is a fascinating one. The chronicles of Franklin's evolution on the subject of American statecraft must be examined to fully appreciate his role as the indispensable founder.

If his role in the creation of our nation is not enough, Franklin's roles as an inventor, scientist, writer and social commentator display a genius that is rarely if ever equaled in the history of our republic. He was a Renaissance man, though not without his shortcomings; what he accomplished, despite those human flaws, is simply astounding by any measure.

Franklin's understanding of fundamental human nature surely fueled his many successes. The same can be said of Walther Elias Disney. For nearly nine decades, from the release of his revolutionary animated classic, *Snow White and the Seven Dwarfs,* to this very day, Disney, and the company he left behind, has dominated the entertainment landscape of America. His work not only redefined animation and movie entertainment but created some of the greatest brands any industry has known as well as a new way for Americans to vacation. If Franklin helped launch the American story, Disney in many ways reinvented it, often sanding off the sharp edges in what was more a tribute to America than a retelling of hard facts.

There is much these men share in common. Not only were they the youngest sons in their respective families, but they both came of age under the imposing hand of patriarchal dominance, in the case of Franklin his older brother, that was neither kind nor nurturing. They both left home at or near age seventeen, each employing a bit of subterfuge in the process. We are the beneficiaries of spirits that could not be stifled or stunted. An examination of these two astonishing lives provides many fascinating parallels and a blueprint for a life lived with purpose. They exceeded all that could reasonably be expected during any life of any age. And to this day, they define a whole lot about who we are as Americans.

Chapter 1

The Conversion of Benjamin Franklin Begins

They that can give up essential liberty to obtain a little temporary safety deserve neither liberty nor safety.

~ B. Franklin

It took time for Benjamin Franklin to conclude that the only path forward for the American colonies was independence. His opinion mattered. Franklin was perhaps the most recognizable of American leaders. He enjoyed a towering status and rose to the rank of a true gentleman, a rarity in the American colonies. By the middle of the eighteenth century a gentleman attained his status by a virtuous rise founded on well-refined manners, superior education, and an unmistakable air of high culture. It was not enough for a man to obtain wealth or independence alone. Likewise, a title or peerage alone did not confer the status of gentleman. The gentleman was required to practice courtesy in all circumstances.

There were few men born in the colonies who would enjoy the status of gentleman and fewer who would enjoy the reputation internationally. Franklin was a proud Briton. His connections to the mother country were an integral part of his well-guarded reputation.

As early as 1762, Franklin enjoyed a reputation as a "celebrity philosopher" and Oxford University awarded him the degree of Doctor of Civil Law at a special convocation. In London he discussed philosophy with notable Enlightenment figures including David Hume and Lord Kames. Franklin dazzled his many British and European friends with his wide array of knowledge and study, including a keen ability to expound on scientific and natural philosophy from the observation of many commonplace things. It seems Franklin's genius and his pride in that significant intellect was best celebrated on a larger and international stage. What Britain and the continent offered, the colonies could not match. Franklin must have reveled in his son William's appointment as the Royal Governor of New Jersey in August 1762. The appointment was followed shortly by the procession and coronation of George III, which the Franklins had planned to attend. Inexplicably, the younger Franklin found himself marching in the procession itself, a circumstance that must have made his father very proud.

It does not require great imagination to conclude that Ben Franklin viewed himself as first and foremost a Briton. His very reputation, especially the international one, was enhanced by his British heritage. As late as 1773, Franklin's view as to a reconciliation between England and the Colonies was not only a hope but also consistent with the great pride he felt as one of the empire's most notable subjects.

Despite his rather strong predilections otherwise, events would soon catch up with Franklin. The winds of change were fanned by Franklin's agency on behalf of first Pennsylvania and later Massachusetts. In 1764 the Pennsylvania Assembly appointed him as its agent to petition the Crown to replace the proprietorship of the Penns with a royal form of government. His second agency, on behalf of Massachusetts, became the more consequential one as circumstances developed.

1 | The Conversion of Benjamin Franklin Begins

Franklin's appointment on behalf of Massachusetts began with correspondence from Thomas Cushing, speaker of the Massachusetts Colonial Assembly, dated November 6, 1770. By the time of that lengthy engagement letter, Massachusetts was fully embroiled in a struggle with the mother country over the imposition of taxation and fees, all supported by the threat of military force. The letter began;

> Province of the Massachusetts Bay
> November. 6th, 1770
>
> Sir
>
> The House of Representatives of this his Majesty's Province, having made Choice of you to appear for them at the Court of Great Britain, as there may be Occasion, it is necessary that you be well informed of the State and Circumstances of the Province, and the Grievances it labours under, the Redress of which will require your utmost Attention and Application.
>
> You are sensible that the British Parliament has of late years thought proper to raise a Revenue in America without our Consent, by divers Laws made expressly for that Purpose: and to dispose of the Monies raised, for the administration of Justice and the Defence of the Colonies: The Reasons and Grounds of our Complaint against these Acts, are so well known and understood by you, that it is needless for us to mention them at this Time.

In 1772 Parliament established that the Massachusetts governor's salary would henceforth be paid and controlled by the Crown. The Massachusetts Assembly protested the tightening grip of royal authority and sent a petition to Franklin asserting that the Assembly and not the Crown controlled the governor's salary as a matter of law. It was left to their agent in London to seek a remedy.

The petition was received by Franklin in November of 1772. Two critical events occurred before the year's end. First, Franklin was convinced by the recently appointed Secretary of State, Lord Dartmouth, not to present the Massachusetts petition. Franklin apparently speculated that a recantation of the petition by the Massachusetts Assembly in light of the new government in London might be well received there.

The second event, of much greater consequence, is at least arguably related to Franklin's expectation as to the disappointment he would engender with the Massachusetts Assembly as a result of the first. On December 2, 1772, Franklin privately corresponded with Speaker of the Massachusetts Assembly, Thomas Cushing, enclosing a series of letters authored between 1767 and 1769 by Massachusetts Royal Governor Thomas Hutchinson, Lt. Governor Andrew Oliver, and others. Those letters comprised correspondence to the by-then deceased British Under Secretary of State Thomas Whatley. On January 5, 1773, Franklin wrote to Cushing: "Sir, I did myself the honour of writing to you on the 2nd of December past, inclosing some *original newspapers to the 30th November last* which I hope got safe to hand."

How Franklin obtained Hutchinson's letters to Whatley remains a mystery. It seems clear that what he sent Cushing were the originals, as Franklin suggested in the draft of his January 5, 1773 letter. On January 11, 1774, when Franklin was summoned before the Privy Council for a hearing on the Massachusetts petition to remove Hutchinson (based in part on the famous letters), the

1 | The Conversion of Benjamin Franklin Begins

Lord President of the Privy Council, Earl Gower, requested the production of the original letters upon which the charge was based. Franklin could only respond that "these copies are attested by several gentlemen at Boston and a notary public." Thus, the location of the originals, consistent with his prior correspondence, was conceded by Franklin.

It seems reasonably clear that Franklin once had in his possession the originals of the letters that were appropriated from the files of Whatley. In his book *The First American,* author H.W. Brands suggests that Franklin did not communicate the nature of any assistance in obtaining the letters to Cushing or anyone else who preserved it for history. The author Thomas Fleming commented on the issue in at least two of his works, the first of which was *Benjamin Franklin: A Biography in His Own Words* (published in 1972 and based on *The Papers of Benjamin Franklin Volume 1-15;* Yale University Press, 1959). In this work, Fleming suggests only that "a friend had shown some letters that Hutchinson and Lieutenant Governor Andrew Oliver had written to Thomas Whatley." Fleming continues that the letters were stolen from Whatley's file subsequent to his death and that Franklin forwarded *copies* to Boston (a statement that dampens confidence as to the depth of Fleming's 1972 research). In his 1997 book *Liberty*, Fleming suggests, without much explanation, "Most historians now think Franklin obtained the letters from a former Governor of Massachusetts, Thomas Pownall."

One of the historians that Fleming was referring to is Bernard Bailyn. In Bailyn's 1974 publication *The Ordeal of Thomas Hutchinson,* he states his belief that it was former Massachusetts Governor Thomas Pownall who gave Franklin the letters. While Bailyn admits his opinion is conjectural, he does indicate it is "powerfully" supported by circumstantial evidence. The theory implicating Pownall is based on the former governor's sympathy for the colony and his desire to return to Massachusetts as a governor, presumably after the removal of Hutchinson as well as the reestablishment of British imperialism itself. The Pownall theory lacks a strong connection to the reasonable expectations of the participants. Could Pownall really expect to be a friend to the colony and reinvigorate British imperialism at the same time? While Bailyn suggests that Pownall was, like Franklin, squarely in the middle of the both sides, there is a clear distinction. Franklin was a colonial agent with only a single fiduciary upon which all his honor was staked.

More recent research contained in Volume 19 of *The Papers of Benjamin Franklin* (published in 1975) points to the dueling John Temple as the "likeliest subject" (*Papers of B.F.* 19: 404, N.2). In correspondence sent by Temple to Franklin in 1781, Temple admitted that it was he who procured the letters for Franklin and placed the conditions upon their use. The admission does lack any corroboration by Franklin himself, since if he replied to the letter the reply has never been found. Nonetheless, there is some corroboration for Temple's confession.

First and foremost, Temple had access to the letters. After the death of his brother Thomas, William Whatley permitted Temple access to Thomas' files for the purpose of retrieving Temple's own correspondence to Thomas Whatley. Temple was alone during part of the time he had that access. Secondly, Temple had motivation to dislike Hutchinson since Temple believed the Governor was responsible for his loss of a customs post in Boston. Additionally, Temple resided in Boston both before and

1 | The Conversion of Benjamin Franklin Begins

after the "Letters Affair" and was known to have local sympathies (*Papers of B.F.* 19:403-306). Another important piece of the puzzle was a duel prompted by accusations concerning the infamous letters.

Temple's solitary access to Thomas Whatley's files in October 1772 became a widespread rumor in London once the theft of the letters became a scandal. As a result, both Temple and William Whatley fell under a cloud of suspicion as potential suspects. The two publicly argued and those arguments led directly to a duel. Temple may have had his honor to save but it is also possible he had much to hide.

While, as previously noted, conventional wisdom has long dictated that Franklin never revealed the source of the Hutchinson letters, new research has challenged that. Maybe Franklin, in a totally Franklinesque fashion, did leave the answer behind. Jeremy John Bell, historian and a performer interpreting eighteenth-century figures, has developed a fascinating theory that concerns the letters that changed history. Bell, who is currently performing a Benjamin Franklin show focused on the tawdry side of our most interesting founder, has uncovered some telling clues.

Bell asserts that an anonymous item published in the *Massachusetts Gazette and Boston Post-Boy* on April 18, 1774, sheds some light on the long-standing mystery. The item is dated February 4, less than a week after Franklin's appearance before the Privy Council to answer for the release of the Hutchinson letters. The letter to the *Gazette* begins:

> The *Public*, as well as the *Privy Council* seem anxious to know how Letters, which have occasioned a *little* Bloodshed, and a great *deal* of Noise, have found their way to America. Were

men to give themselves the trouble of inquiring properly in *Crane court,* they would find the true reason in the form of *Philosophical Transactions* of that Place. A *certain* Doctor is the intimate Friend of a *certain* Baronet; a certain Baronet has access to a *certain* House not a hundred miles from one of the gates of St. James Park. *Certain* Letters might lie upon a *certain* Table; and it is most *certain* that such Letters might be *certainly* Conveyed, without any *Electrical Shock* on the part of the worthy Baronet into the hand of his Philosophical friend...

Bell explains that the letter to the *Gazette* was written contemporaneously with other letters to different newspapers known to be written by Franklin.

According to Bell, the *Gazette* item contains a number of strong connections to Franklin. The baronet referred to in the piece is Sir Francis Dashwood, says Bell, who goes on to point out that Dashwood and Franklin were close friends. Moreover, Dashwood stood with Franklin when he was summonsed to appear before the Privy Council. One of the most fascinating clues Bell points out concerns the phrase, "that such letters might be conveyed without any Electrical Shock." It turns out the baronet had a large wooden structure installed on the top of a church constructed on his estate. The bell tower room was large enough to accommodate six people and Bell notes it was equipped with a lightning rod installed by the inventor of the same, Dr. Benjamin Franklin. Dashwood, as a gentleman, former member of Parliament and postmaster general, is certainly the type of Briton who could have had access to the letters and an opportunity to convey them to his friend, Doctor Franklin.

1 | The Conversion of Benjamin Franklin Begins

Bell further supports his theory with language from the accusation against Franklin in the Privy Council, particularly the charge of being "the Prime Conductor of the whole contrivance" of the purloined letters. The anonymous piece sent to the *Gazette*, beyond the talk of being a safe remove from electrical shock, stated, "it will however be extremely shocking should both, for their services to the people, be turned out from their office under the Crown." Bell notes how fond Franklin was of word games and riddles. The word game in the *Gazette* piece is just the type of hijinks Franklin would have enjoyed. Bell's case is compelling.

However Franklin came into possession of these original letters, a number of points remain clear: the exhortation of Hutchinson, whatever the context, that "there must be an abridgement of what is called British Liberty" would serve as ample fodder for the colonial propagandists; Franklin, deeply upset by the letters, perceived that Hutchinson distorted the colonial circumstances to gain personal favor in London and his eventual Royal Governorship; and Franklin understood the seriousness of transgression in sending the documents back to Boston.

Various reasons have been advanced as to why Franklin dealt in the letters. One motivation attributed to Franklin was that the underlying nature of the correspondence was public and consisted of the discourse between public officers as concerns public policy. (This is an argument more suited to a modern-day Freedom of Information Act request, but hardly supportable by eighteenth-century standards). Another possibility advanced was that Franklin held a suspicion that his own mail as a colonial agent was being examined by the authority of the British Secretary of State. Some of Franklin's letters had arrived with seals appearing to have been broken and resealed. Whatever the reason, Franklin was clearly engaged in one of the first acts of American espionage. Franklin's pragmatic moralism would particularly suit him to the demands placed on a spy. He was also quite aware of being spied upon, not only by the examination of his own mail but also by the recitation of his private letters to the Assembly.

Despite any measure of good faith and his role as a conciliator, Franklin's attitude was rapidly changing, especially during the latter part of 1773. Franklin the mediator was becoming Franklin the propagandist, man of international intrigue and ultimately the revolutionary who saw only one course. The shift in attitude was in no small part created by the chain of events that placed the Hutchinson letters in Thomas Cushing's hands in early 1773. Franklins original instruction to Cushing was to allow the letters to "be seen by some men of worth in the province for their satisfaction only." Franklin also advised Cushing that he, Franklin, was not, according to the instructions he had received, permitted to publish the letters in England or allow copies of the documents to be made. Franklin also retained temporary possession of the documents ultimately expecting the return of the originals.

While Franklin may have never reasonably expected that the letters would escape publication in Massachusetts, it is quite conceivable that he believed his role in the affair could be kept secret. The express instructions to Cushing included the showing of the correspondence to the more radical Bostonians such as James Otis, Samuel Adams and John Hancock. The propaganda value of these letters to the Boston radicals could not have been lost on Franklin. The supplying of these letters without their eventual publication would, under the circumstances, have been no different than placing the proverbial hungry man before a feast and requesting that he not eat. Prior to Franklin's knowledge of the publication of the letters in Massachusetts, at least one complaint about the non-publication caveat was answered by Franklin in his letter to Samuel Cooper:

> You mention the surprize of gentlemen whom those letters have been communicated, at the restrictions with which they were accompanied, and which they suppose render them incapable of answering any important end. The great reason of forbidding their publication, was an apprehension that it might put all the possessors of such correspondence here upon their guard, and so prevent the obtaining more of it. (*Papers of B.F.*, July 7, 1773).

Franklin concludes the paragraph regarding restrictions with the following: "However this may be, the terms given with them could only be those with which they were received" (*Papers of B.F.*, July 7, 1773). Franklin had also informed Cushing that he would have published the letters himself if he was permitted. It seems overwhelmingly clear that while Franklin was scrupulously observing the instructions of that mysterious person or persons who placed these letters in his possession, he knew and even implied what the ultimate result would be. To expand on the prior analogy, Franklin not only seated the hungry man before the feast and instructed him not to eat but also left the room.

Chapter 2

The Letter Affair

The first mistake in public business is the going into it.

~ B. Franklin

Franklin's political identity during 1773 is a complex and interesting study. While he did not want to disappoint the more radical colonials, especially after obtaining his unofficial ambassador status from them, he certainly was not completely in their school of thought. Nonetheless, the conciliator was becoming less conciliatory with the passage of time. His own satirical pieces in London's *Public Advertiser*, "Rules by which a Great Empire May Be Reduced to a Small One" and "An edict by the King of Prussia," both published in September 1773, hinted at the building ire Franklin was experiencing. The content of the Hutchinson letters was troubling to Franklin. He thought exposing Hutchinson as the true culprit in worsening relations between the colonies and the mother country might aid in a reconciliation. That plan would ultimately fall flat. On the contrary, the letters and the revelation of Franklin's part in their publication would forever end his role as a peacemaker.

Franklin's involvement in obtaining and publishing the Hutchinson letters remained a secret until Christmas Day 1773. Franklin desired that his role remain secret despite his suggestions to the contrary. Thomas Cushing informed Franklin about the Massachusetts Assembly's publication of the letters in June 1773. In Franklin's reply to Cushing on July 25, 1773, he confirms receipt of Cushing's correspondence and then notes the issue of secrecy.

> I observe you mention, that no person besides Dr. Cooper and one of the committee know they came from me. I did not accompany them with any request of being myself conceal'd, for believing what I did to be in the way of my duty as Agent, tho' I had no doubt of its giving offence, not only to the parties expos'd, but to the administration here, I was regardless of the consequences. However, since the letters themselves are now copied and printed, contrary to the promise I made, I am glad my name has not been heard on the occasion; and as I do not see it could be of any use to the publick, I now wish it may continue unknown- tho' I hardly expect it (*Papers of B.F.*, July 25, 1773).

Had Franklin's involvement been made public earlier, even without the intervening "Tea Party," it seems doubtful that he could have continued his service as Massachusetts' colonial agent. His utility in counseling both sides of the dispute relative to moderation, thoughtful consideration and reconsideration, could not have continued. Ultimately, three events would converge to make any reconciliation impossible even to the optimistic Franklin. First, the tempest surrounding the publication of the letters had led to accusations regarding their theft in which Whatley's brother implicated John Temple, a government official and known colonial sympathizer. Temple challenged Whatley to a duel in which Whatley was wounded. Subsequently, upon hearing charges that his tactics were unfair, Temple announced that the feud was unsettled. More violence was anticipated.

Fearing that, Franklin sent a letter to the *London Chronicle* indicating that the combatants were both "totally ignorant and innocent" and "I alone am the person who obtained and transmitted to Boston the letters in question." The dramatic admission would seal Franklin's diplomatic fate. No longer could he be effective as a colonial ambassador or the agent of compromise. Whether Franklin, who was candid when the admission was made, ever wanted to give it, is suspect. The accusations, charges and duel between Temple and Whatley must have been quite public in nature. The fact that Franklin only made the admission after blood was spilled and more violence threatened seems to underscore how much he wanted the secret kept.

The second event, the Boston "Tea Party" was an occurrence that Franklin could not have anticipated to coincide with his public examination concerning his part in the theft of the Hutchinson letters. In fact, his first summons to the Privy Council on January 11, 1774, was before news of the Tea Party had yet arrived in London. Although Franklin was surprised by the invitation to hear the Massachusetts petition to dismiss by then-even-more-despised Hutchinson, no one believed the petition would be given genuine consideration. The real purpose of the hearing was to deal with the petitioners and their agent. The hearing was postponed to permit Franklin an opportunity, which he deliberated on forgoing, to secure legal counsel. Franklin asked for and was granted three weeks, which reinforces the conclusion of the coincidental nature of ensuing events.

On January 22, 1774, the *St. James Chronicle* published the first news of the Tea Party in London. On January 27, 1774, Lord North received an official report concerning the Tea Party from Governor Hutchinson. A meeting of the cabinet was convened to discuss the government's response. Two days later, on January 29, 1774, the Privy Council hearing was reconvened with a new urgency and vehemence that did not bode well for Dr. Franklin.

Franklin's own disdain for Hutchinson led him to conclude that once exposed, the self-serving governor would be removed for the common good of the empire. His plan thoroughly backfired. Wedderburn charged Franklin as "the first mover and prime conductor of this whole contrivance against His Majesty's two Governors; and having help of his own special confidents and party leaders, first made the (Massachusetts) Assembly his Agents in carrying on his own secret designs."

Wedderburn's blistering diatribe continued for an hour. The Solicitor General's oration included innuendo, sarcasm and pointed attacks. Wedderburn assailed the violation of private correspondence by Franklin:

> These are the letters which Dr. Franklin treats as public letters, and has thought proper to secrete them for his own private purpose. How he got them, or in whose hands they were at the time of Mr. Whatley's death, the Doctor has not yet thought proper to tell us. Till he do, he wittingly leaves the world at liberty to conjecture about them as they please, and to reason upon those conjectures.

The attack was personal and Wedderburn forged ahead with insult upon insult.

2 | The Letter Affair

> These are the lessons taught in Dr. Franklin's school of Politics. My Lords, I do not say that Dr. Franklin is the original author of the book. But your Lordships will give me leave to observe, in the first place, that it is not very likely, that any of the Doctor's scholars at Boston, should attempt to draw up such a state of rights and grievances, when the *great man,* their master, had given them notice that he should himself set about the work: and, in the next place, that if the Doctor should not chuse now to filiate the child, yet the time has been when he was not ashamed of it; for, after it had had its operation in America, the Doctor reprinted it here, with a preface of his own, and presented it to his friends.

Throughout, Franklin remained emotionless and quiet. The description of his demeanor, in light of his great mental acuity, can only be interpreted as purposeful. His stoicism concealed a tempest. Franklin was far too great an intellect and possessor of emotional strength to give up anything of his full thoughts or demonstrate the effect of what the observers deemed unparalleled. Edmund Burke characterized the proceedings as being outside "all bounds and measures." Many of the observers "laughed and cheered at the solicitor's slashing assault on Franklin's behavior and character." Edward Bancroft, then a friend of Franklin and fledgling diplomat headed for a career as a double agent during the Revolution, observed the Privy Council attack. "The Doctor was dressed in a full dress suit of spotted Manchester velvet, and previously composed, so as to afford a place of tranquil expression of countenance, and he did not suffer the slightest alteration of it to appear during the continuance of the speech in which he was so harshly and improperly treated. In short, to quote the words which he employed concerning himself on another occasion, he kept his 'countenance as immoveable as if his features had been made of wood.'"

On February 15, 1774, Franklin wrote a lengthy letter to Cushing describing what he endured in the cockpit of the Privy Council. Included in his response was a justification as concerns the now-famous letters:

> In truth I came by them honourably, and my intention in sending them was virtuous, if an endeavor to lessen the breach between two states of the same empire be such, by showing that the injuries complained of by one of them did not proceed from the other, but from traitors among themselves (*Papers of B.F.,* February 15, 1774).

Franklin mused further and described the hopelessness of the circumstances:

> It may be supposed that I am very angry on this occasion, and therefore I did purpose to add no reflections of mine on the treatment the Assembly and their agent have received, lest they should be thought the effects of resentment and desire of exasperating. But indeed what I feel on my own account is half lost in what I feel for the publick. When I see, that all petitions and complaints of grievances are so odious to government, that even the mere pipe which conveys them becomes obnoxious, I am at a loss to know how peace and union are to be maintained or restored between the different parts of the empire. Grievances cannot be redressed unless they are known; and they cannot be known but through complaints

and petitions: If these are deemed affronts, and the messengers punished as offenders, who will henceforth send petitions? And who will deliver them? It has been thought a dangerous thing in any state to stop up the vent of griefs. Wise governments have therefore generally received petitions with some indulgence, even when but slightly founded. Those, who think themselves injured by their rulers, are sometimes, by a mild and prudent answer, convinced of their errour. But where complaining is a crime, hope becomes despair (*Papers of B.F.*, February 15, 1774).

Franklin's efforts at reconciliation had failed. His attempts exhibited an interest in compromise and a genuine belief that corrupt officials such as Hutchinson had inflamed the controversies shamelessly for self-gain and needlessly to the detriment of both sides. Franklin hoped the exposure of Hutchinson would give both sides a better perspective. In fact, the exposure of Hutchinson revealed much more than Franklin had ever bargained for. What Franklin came to learn was that the divide between Britain and her colonies was as wide as the difference between his thoughts and motivations and those of Hutchinson. Franklin came, later than some, to the ultimate conclusion. But conclude he did. His philosophical arrival given who he was, to contemporaries on both sides of the Atlantic, signaled a new political reality and a defining event in American history.

Chapter 3

Walt Disney Discovers Television

I don't consider myself an actor or anything but in trying to get hold of things, I can introduce them, get them going. I'm myself, good or bad, I'm still myself, that will be the gimmick.

~ Walt Disney

Like Franklin, Walt Disney was responsible for many innovations. Both men shared a keen sense of observation and willingness to imagine new and better ways of doing things. Coming to the conclusion that a particular item or process needs improvement is one thing, but committing to the change necessary to accomplish it is quite another. Both Franklin and Disney had a number of seminal moments during their lives. Selecting a pinnacle for either man is a difficult thing.

If the "letters affair" and its impact on the course of the American Revolution has at least a claim as the singular moment in Franklin's life, television has a solid place atop Walt Disney's trajectory through the world of entertainment. For Walt, television was one of those advancements that had to have been understood from the perspective of a decade into the future. All of Disney's success has a common thread – staying ahead of the curve with an uncanny perception of what would succeed in the years to come. Doing it better, while important, was not enough. Disney constantly strove to do it differently as well.

Television attracted Walt's attention as early as 1939, the year the fledging industry took flight in America. RCA created an exhibition for the New York World's Fair that year in Flushing Meadows, New York. On April 30, 1939, RCA debuted the first commercial and publicly accessible television broadcast. Franklin D. Roosevelt became the first US president to appear on television that historic day and RCA began selling its television sets the very next day. The company's sets ranged in size from five to twelve inches and sold at prices between $200 and $1,000.

None of this was lost on Walt Disney, who understood the potential impact of the new medium on entertainment. As early as October 28, 1939, Walt authored a memo to his brother Roy (the man with a close eye on the business side of the Disney business) and the Disney legal department. Walt noted, "Everything we do in the future should include television rights. There might be a big angle on television for shows we have ready produced." No words could have been more prophetic.

In May 1939, and before its theatrical release, NBC aired Disney's short cartoon film *Donald's Cousin Gus*, as a test within its brand-new and very limited broadcast system. In the late 1930s, Great Britain's BBC was the leader of the pioneering days of commercial television, well ahead of RCA and NBC in the United States. Television coverage of the coronation of King George VI and Wimbledon in 1937 led to the sale of 9,000 television sets in Great Britain. All of that progress came to a screeching halt in 1939 when the BBC suspended broadcasts as a result of the Second World War. When the BBC went off the air it was in the midst of broadcasting Disney's *Mickey's Gala Premier* produced in 1933. When

3 | Walt Disney Discovers Television

the BBC resumed its broadcasts on V-E Day in 1945, it returned by airing the same Disney cartoon at the precise spot it was cut off in 1939 when its broadcasts were abruptly ended.

By 1944 RCA was entreating Walt Disney to become a pitchman of sorts in an effort to market the company's television sets. At the time, movie studios did not support the new medium and quality programming was hard to come by. In relatively limited production, television sets were expensive and overall distribution was quite small. RCA needed a way to promote its sets and turned to one of the country's most creative forces. RCA wanted Walt Disney to produce an infomercial titled "The World in Your Living Room." While the piece never got produced, it did cause Disney to deepen his company's attention to and research into television.

Within four years of the infomercial proposal, Walt Disney had concluded that television presented a significant opportunity to promote Disney films. Walt hired C. J. LaRoche, a think-tank firm to study the impact of television on the Walt Disney Company. The outside researchers issued a report titled "Television for Walt Disney Productions" in September 1950. The report findings outlined both the financial exposure and long-term benefits of television to Disney. Two months later the Disney studio announced it would produce the company's very first television special.

The decision of Disney studios to enter the world of television, especially in retrospect, was monumental in nature, not just for the Walt Disney Company but for the whole of American culture. There were a number of fascinating aspects surrounding Disney's pioneering television effort. The special would cost $100,000 to produce. It was one of the most expensive television shows produced up until that time. Bill Walsh, the man tapped to produce the show, worried out load that he had no experience in the new medium. Walt replied, "Who does?"

Contrary to most in the motion picture industry, Walt saw television as a co-marketing opportunity not a competitor. The idea of promoting Disney films on television was put to an immediate application in the special. At the time, the release of *Alice in Wonderland* was imminent, and Walt was eager to use the television show to market it. The show started a long tradition of Walt Disney serving as an amiable television host, enlarging an already transcendent entertainment personality. Yet in that very first special, which would ultimately air on Christmas Day 1950, Walt was a bit concerned about going it alone. Walt recruited Edgar Bergen, a close friend and radio star famous for his ventriloquist dummy "Charlie McCarthy," to cohost the Christmas special. Astonishingly, Walt was hesitant to host the show solo and adding Bergen to the billing provided him a measure of comfort.

The special was originally scheduled to air on CBS, but when the infant network could not guarantee enough stations to carry it, the show's sponsor, Coca-Cola, yanked it. Instead, the special aired on NBC with a guarantee of 62 affiliate stations. NBC made television history when the special opened with "Coca-Cola brings you holiday greetings!" against an image of Santa Claus standing before a Christmas tree with his huge sack of Christmas toys, complete with strategically placed Minnie Mouse and Donald Duck dolls on top. Mickey was already under the Christmas tree.

The special was a huge success, pairing two of the world's most recognizable brands, Coca-Cola and Disney.

3 | Walt Disney Discovers Television

And though the distribution of television sets in the United States still had a long way to go, the special captured 90% of the viewing audience that Christmas afternoon. It is estimated that the Christmas extravaganza drew 20 million viewers gathered before virtually all of the country's 10.5 million television sets. By the time Disneyland would open in California five years later, the number of television sets in America would eclipse 30 million, reaching 65% of the country's households. In 1961, nearly a decade before Disney World opened in Florida, 90% of the households in the country would own a television set.

Walt was convinced and he let his stockholders in on his views in the Disney Company's 1950 annual report.

> I regard television as one of our most important channels for the development of a new motion picture audience. Millions of tele-viewers never go to a picture theater, and countless others infrequently. As a promotion medium, however, television has gained maturity as most top sales executives in the nation have recognized. We all can remember when the prophets of doom predicted radio would ruin the film industry. Instead it turned into one of our greatest selling forces.

The Christmas special was both a confirmation and extension of Walt's long-held beliefs about the television medium. Walt's fascination with television went back as early as the mid-1930s. In those days, he traveled to Camden, New Jersey, to meet with RCA's David Sarnoff and take in a demonstration of the new medium. Walt was impressed enough to negotiate the retention of television rights when his studio left United Artists to sign a new distribution agreement with RKO in 1936. Ten years later, the Disney studio applied for a television license from the FCC with the intention of building a broadcasting center on the studio lot. Roy Disney killed the idea, fearing both the expense and preferring to wait until the technology included color broadcasting, something that would fit the animation genre best.

Unlike most studio executives who feared the new medium, Walt and his finance-conscious brother Roy embraced it. They both saw not only the promotional value of television for their film offerings but also the value of the new medium as a testing ground for new material. The Disney brothers also knew that content-hungry television networks were an ideal place to recycle older films and shorts. Disney was particularly well poised to take full advantage of television. Others noticed too. In the wake of the 1950 Christmas special, Jack Gould of *The New York Times* wrote, "Walt Disney can take over television anytime he likes." Gould praised the special as "one of the most engaging and charming programs of the year."

Television was clearly in need of content and the Disney Studio (an early name for Walt Disney Productions) was uniquely positioned to provide the type of programming audiences would enjoy. Despite what seemed like the most natural of fits, there were still a few hurdles to clear, not the least of which was Disney committing to the rigors of producing regular programing. The idea of producing regular programming in the early 1950s was still novel and forays with networks and sponsors were not without fits and starts.

Nonetheless, television and Walt Disney Productions were on parallel trajectories. The resulting union would put an indelible stamp on of the future of American culture. The eventual collaboration would not only involve films and other content but the creation of a theme park that would change the way Americans took their vacations and entertained themselves.

Chapter 4

Walt Disney's Formative Years

That's the real problem with the world, too many people grow up.

~ Walt Disney

Walt Disney and Benjamin Franklin were, beyond any doubt, creative geniuses. They share the happy concurrence of leaving a legacy of achievement that defies comparison. All Walt Disney did was to create a new cinematic art form, win more Academy Awards than anyone in history, and be recognized as a genius before reaching age forty with honorary degrees from both Harvard and Yale. Before reaching age thirty, Disney built a media and entertainment company without rival in the world and established highly recognizable brands and characters that few or any could equal or eclipse. Before he was done, he invented a new American vacation that showcased his lifetime achievements. To this day his theme parks continue to evolve with improvements, or "plussing" as he called it, more than six decades after his death.

Franklin too boasts a very long list of accomplishments. As a talented writer and student of human nature, he authored political pieces, including the first political cartoon published in America, as well as entertainment pieces, most notably *Poor Richard's Almanac*. He was the only founding father to sign the Declaration of Independence, the Peace of Paris and the US Constitution. As an inventor he studied electricity and other natural phenomena, leading to a bevy of inventions including the lightening rod, the Franklin stove (to increase the efficiency of fireplaces), and bifocals. He was the first postmaster general of the United States and the leading force in the creation of several organizations aimed to positively benefit society. These included the founding of the University of Pennsylvania, creating the Junto Club (also known as the Leather Apron Club) to harness and share learning among tradesmen, and establishing the first lending library in America.

Disney and Franklin shared an intense drive to achieve. Many creative thinkers are beset by mood disorders. There is little doubt that Walt Disney suffered bouts of depression and profound sadness throughout his life. While most scholars do not believe that Franklin had any significant mental illness, he did preoccupy himself with the attainment of virtue and healthy living models of both the mind and the body. Franklin also invented the glass "armonica," which he instructed could be manipulated to treat melancholy with pleasing tones. Like Disney, Franklin had significant tensions within his immediate family both as a lad and later in life. Neither man could escape some measure of impact on their psyche from the relationships they experienced. Though they lived in far different worlds, much about human nature does not change and both men were shaped by experiences that they could not fully control. Whatever the era or century, history yields many examples of great thinkers who have been burdened by depression. From Van Gogh to Mark Twain, or Charles Dickens, Mozart, and Nikola Tesla, there is a long list of those who achieved at the highest levels while battling the darkest moods.

The question is often asked: do those with mood disorders possess special talents and heightened creativity or does the exercise of genius come at a price? A 2012 study by *Perspective on Psychological Science* examined that issue and published the results as a journal article, "Creativity and Mood Disorder: A Systematic Review and Meta-Analysis." The study was not conclusive. The author, Christa L. Taylor of the State University of New York at Albany, theorized that examining whether "creativity is related to mood disorder is too general to yield constructive answers and may lead to faulty or overgeneralized conclusions."

It would appear that creativity may be an outlet for those suffering from a variety of mood disorders. In some cases those deepest influences may find a measure of calm from cutting-edge achievement. It may also be equally likely that the intensity of a nonstop lifestyle may take its toll when patterns of sleep and food consumption change and periods of hyperactivity are present.

Walt Disney endured more than his share of dark moods. At least some of that darkness may have been related to his desire to not only create and innovate at a heady pace but to control the environment around him. Disney biographer Neal Gabler, in his 2006 book *Walt Disney: The Triumph of the American Imagination,* captured one of Walt's darkest moments in 1931, at a time when the nation was struggling with its own turmoil.

> But if the Depression did not affect Walt economically, it was in many ways replicated in his own emotional depression. Just at the nation

could not escape the economic buffets, Walt could not secure his fantasy world against the assaults of the real world, could not, in fact, make it perfect enough or impregnable enough, which led to his breakdown.

The flash point of his breakdown was his wife Lillian's miscarriage. At first Walt fended off any concerns in the wake of the sad end to Lillian's first pregnancy, insisting he was fine. He wasn't fine. "I had one hell of a breakdown. I went to pieces," Walt later said. He couldn't get through a phone conversation without breaking down into tears. He was a wreck and he knew changes needed to be made.

The immediate crisis was met by Walt's doctor, who recommended a vacation. Walt and Lillian took a train from California to Washington, DC, where they spent three days before moving on to Key West, again by train. They traveled to Havana on a tug and stayed at the Hotel Nacional before taking a cruise ship home via the Panama Canal. Once home, Walt attempted to balance his grueling work schedule with exercise at the Hollywood Athletic Club and engaging in a variety of sports. These activities—ice skating, swimming, houseback riding and boxing—were new to Walt and not part of a childhood routine that had been more about service to his father.

Elias Disney was, to be kind, a stern taskmaster. Nearly all of Walt's childhood was compressed into nearly five happy years the family spent on a farm in Marceline, Missouri. It was how Walt chose to remember his formative years. The idyllic days in small-town America were where he retreated mentally though most of his youth. The great majority of his youth was spent either in Chicago or Kansas City, involuntarily tied to his father's business ventures that never seemed to pan out even when the labor was nearly free. One case in point: Elias bought a paper route in Kansas City after the family moved from Marceline. Eighteen-year-old Roy and ten-year-old Walt delivered the 650 papers twice a day. Too exhausted for real attention to his studies, Walt was not a good student. Walt got paid, according to Roy, some "small amount," and Roy received three dollars per week. There was no mistake about it, Walt was in service to his father and would remain so until he was able to leave home. In relative terms, Marceline represented Walt's carefree days of youth. As those memories became more distant, they became all the more important to Walt. He never forgot Marceline and the time would come when those memories took a form far more tangible than mere reflections of a nostalgic past.

As difficult as Elias was, the Disney family remained close. In business, Roy and Walt worked together for life, each taking on far different roles, but almost always complementing each other with their different talents. Their older brothers Herbert and Raymond were never involved in the Disney business. Herbert was a postman and lived an infinitely more simple life than his younger brothers. When he retired, Walt announced he envied Herbert's life, saying, "I'd give a lot for a little of it, and believe me, I mean it." Elias and Flora's second son, Raymond was originally named Walter until his parents reconsidered. Ray, like Herbert, declined an offer to join the Disney brothers' fledging studio. Instead, Ray built a successful insurance business in Los Angeles and counted among his clients the Disney Bros. Studio, which later became Walt Disney Productions. He remained close to his brothers and was an advisor from time to time. Like his younger brother Walt, Ray was fascinated by Abraham Lincoln and even contributed to the creation of the 1964-65 New York World's Fair's Illinois Pavilion, "Great Moments with Mr. Lincoln."

Walt's youngest sibling and only sister, Ruth Flora Disney, was two years younger than him. With proximity in age, the two youngest Disney children formed a close bond. While in Marceline, Walt was held back two years in school so that he and Ruth could attend school together. Ruth lived a private life but she remained close to her brothers. She settled in Portland, Oregon, following her oldest brother Herbert, who resided there until he later moved to California. Ruth married Ted Beecher of Portland in 1934. Ruth and Walt were frequent correspondents and their letters provide an interesting glimpse into the doings of Walt's company through the years. Walt remained committed to Ruth throughout his life and provided her with financial support, as Roy and he did with their other siblings.

The brothers' generosity with their family is also the prelude to a great tragedy. The sad circumstances also open a window to Walt's very different relationship with each of his parents. In 1937 Walt and Roy bought their parents a home in North Hollywood at 4605 Placidia Avenue. The sons were fulfilling a promise to their parents made in connection with their fiftieth wedding anniversary. In assessing the house's attributes, Roy noted, "more important it has a good hearing system." Those words must have long echoed as the heating system began to malfunction soon after the purchase. Flora was told by her housekeeper, "We better get this furnace fixed or else someday we'll wake up and find ourselves dead." Despite a visit by a studio repairman to repair it, that's exactly what happened. On November 16, 1938, Flora got up to use the bathroom and collapsed. She could not be revived and died of carbon monoxide poisoning. Elias survived.

His mother's death was emotionally debilitating, perhaps the most distressing event Walt Disney ever endured. He never talked about her in public again. Some theorize that Flora's death accounts for a spate of post-1938 Disney films featuring motherless children. Whatever the case, the tragedy changed Walt and with it came a time of profound sadness—things would never be the same again.

Elias Disney died on September 13, 1941. Roy called his brother Walt, who was in South America enjoying the warmth of the people and escaping the rigors and ire of a strike at the studio. Roy had thought it best to get his brother out of town until the labor matter was resolved. The situation had grown volatile and Walt's emotions were flaring. Roy knew having Walt around was not going to be productive in ending the labor stoppage.

The striking Disney workers returned three days after Elias's death. Walt did not return for his father's funeral. A chapter was closed, ending a lifetime of tension. As a younger man, Elias had preached stern sermons at a Congregational church. When Elias finally got around to permanently attaching the given name Walter to one of his children, it was the would-be artist son who became Walter Elias Disney. He was named for a Congregationalist minister, Walter Parr. The boy grew up neither stern nor preaching but disagreeing with a father who saw his passions as frivolous.

If there was a distinct turning point in the relationship between Walt and Elias, it was marked by leaving

Marceline. Walt's wife Lillian would say, "Marceline was the most important part of Walt's life. He didn't live there very long. He lived in Chicago and Kansas City much longer. But there was something about the farm that was very important to him." Those were Walt's days of childhood fascination and wonder. He tended the farm's livestock and played in the fields and orchards. He fished and swam in the nearby creek. When he explored, his first pet, a Maltese terrier, tagged along. He spent hours clowning with his friends, his sense of humor shining through, and he spent hours held rapt by stories of brave exploits told by a neighbor and Civil War veteran Erastus Taylor. The bucolic farm days came to an end when Elias caught either typhoid or diphtheria and falling crop prices squeezed the family financially. Elias's farming days in Marceline lasted a mere five years, days Walt never forgot.

When the family moved from Marceline to Kansas City, Elias got angrier. His stern, straight and narrow attitude became even more pronounced. His temper quickened and his autocratic domination left no doubt who was in charge. If his motivation was to protect his family, it was in stark contrast to his youngest son's zest for a happy life.

Though Marceline passed into memory, its importance would never fade for Walt. The memory of Marceline was not only a place he could retreat to but in time it would represent some of his deepest feelings, ones that he could share. Those five years of childhood, years Walt Disney cherished, would someday change the world.

Chapter 5

Of Indenture and Escape

Lost time is never found again.

~ B. Franklin

Benjamin Franklin's autocratic guiding hand was not the product of his father alone but mostly imposed by his brother James, a printer to whom was indentured at age twelve. Franklin was drawn to both books and the sea, and his father, fearing the consequences of the latter, decided the answer was to place his young son in his brother's print shop. In his autobiography, Franklin recounted the circumstances of his vocational fate.

> This bookish inclination at length determined my father to make me a printer, though he had already one son (James) of that profession. In 1717 my brother James, returned from England with a press and letters to set up his business in Boston. I liked it much better than that of my father, but still had a hankering for the sea. To prevent the apprehended effect of such inclination, my father was impatient to have me bound to my brother. I stood out sometime, but at last was persuaded and signed the indenture, when I was yet but twelve years old.

Ben's indenture bound him to his brother until he was twenty-one years old, and he would receive a journeyman's wage for only the last year. The printing business and the resulting access to books permitted the young Franklin to educate himself. The literary exposure added quite measurably to his formal education, which ended when he was ten years old. His writing skill became so proficient that he was able to contribute to his brother's newspaper, the *New England Courant,* secretly under the pseudonym Silence Dogood. As Dogood, Franklin posed as a middle-aged widow. As a result, the sixteen-year-old Franklin was able to publish his work, something James refused to do for his younger brother without resorting to the elaborate ruse.

James was jealous of his young brother and the apprentice suffered much abuse at his master's hand. If Walt had Elias to contend with, Ben had his brother James. In his autobiography, Franklin recounted his poor treatment.

> Though a brother, he considered himself as my master and me as his apprentice, and accordingly expected the same services from me as he would from another; while I thought he degraded me too much in some he required of me, who from a brother expected more indulgence. Our disputes were often brought before our father, and I fancy I was either generally in the right or else a better pleader, because the judgment was generally in my favour. But my brother was passionate and had often beaten me, which I took extremely amiss. I fancy his harsh and tyrannical treatment of me might be a means of impressing me with that aversion to arbitrary power that has stuck

to me through my whole life. Thinking my apprenticeship very tedious, I was continually wishing for some opportunity of shortening it, which at length offered in a manner unexpected.

Before long, James got himself in a bit of a bind that had nothing to do with the managing of his apprentice. In his autobiography, Franklin reveals "one of the pieces in our newspaper on some political point which I have now forgotten, gave offence to the assembly." James was jailed for a month and was prohibited from printing the *New England Courant.* That created an immediate dilemma for the printer; he could change the name of the newspaper but to do so would squander all of the goodwill built up in the newspaper's title. The elder Franklin hatched a scheme. He would put the newspaper in Benjamin's name, and, to avoid any charge of the move being a mere artifice, he formally and publicly discharged his brother's indenture. What the public didn't know, however, was that James promptly required his younger brother to sign new papers of indenture for the remainder of the term. The new indenture was of course kept secret.

Soon after the contrivance was complete, "a fresh difference" arose between the brothers. Benjamin considered asserting his freedom, thinking his brother could not risk making the secret indenture public, but it was not in him to assert his advantage. Franklin deemed his hesitation one of the "first errata of my life," especially when he considered the abuse he suffered as his brother's servant. When Franklin's desire to take his leave became known to his brother, James made sure he could not obtain employment in the Boston printing trade.

Josiah Franklin sided with James on the question of Ben's leaving and the apprentice concluded, "if I attempted to go openly, means would be used to prevent me." With his friend Collins, the seventeen-year-old Franklin concocted a scheme to get out of town. Thus, with a meager sum of money from the sale of his books, Collins arranged Ben's passage on a ship to New York, telling the captain that his friend "had had an intrigue with a girl of bad character."

Walt too did his own plotting to get away from the controlling patriarch in his life. Walt moved from Kansas City to Chicago in 1917 so Elias could take up a hands-on role with the O-Zell Company there. O-Zell was a jelly and fruit juice company in which Elias had made a significant investment. In Chicago Walt enrolled as a freshman at McKinley High School, where he drew for *The McKinley Voice,* the school newspaper. When summer came, he took a job at O-Zell preparing shipping containers and processing apples for pectin, an ingredient necessary to make jelly. Though his artistic talents were put to use at least occasionally at O-Zell, Walt didn't last there. Instead, he took a job at the post office as a substitute mail carrier.

As the summer came to a close, returning to school was not an option for Walt. He told the principal he was "disgusted" by his year at McKinley, and in writing no less. Without any new plans and no desire to return to his father's employment, Walt needed as escape.

The war in Germany preoccupied Americans in 1918 and Walt Disney was no exception. As for many young men throughout the ages, enlisting in the military was a convenient way to get out of town and escape their current circumstances. As always, the lure of adventure was part of the attraction. Unfortunately for Walt, he was too young to sign up. Nonetheless, Walt and his friend Russell Maas tried to sign up for the army. They were just sixteen and were rejected for being under the required age of eighteen. Maas had another plan. He suggested the duo join the American Red Cross ambulance corps, which permitted boys as young as seventeen to enlist. Still a year too young, they were not out of the woods (or the country) yet.

They needed their parents to sign induction papers certifying their ages. Elias refused, saying, "I might be signing your death warrant." Flora was no less concerned about her son's well-being. Walt begged her and she feared if she didn't relent by signing, he would simply run off to some other fate. She signed certifying a birthdate of December 6, 1901, still one year too young. Once the document was notarized, Walt altered it to change the birth date from 1901 to 1900. Presto, he was now old enough to be shipped out to France and for duty mopping up the war front. Disney and his fellow ambulance corps enlistees arrived in Cherbourg, France, nearly three weeks after the armistice was signed.

Like Franklin's escape from Boston, it was more than a geographical separation for Walt. Both men had reached an age where they had to establish themselves away from a dominant hand that could never countenance their intellectual growth and independence. It was a hard lesson for them both, but there was no turning back. There would be no welcome home to regroup from a false start, no safety net and no bailout if they fell flat on their faces.

Both of these young men, though separated by a vast span of the American republic's history, possessed a drive to succeed and a visceral knowledge of what their fellow Americans felt, thought, and wanted. They would need it. Their starts would not be easy. They would have to summon an ample store of faith and perseverance. All those who succeed require more than ideas and genius; Benjamin Franklin and Walt Disney were no different.

Chapter 6

The Early Trials and Tribulations of Franklin and Disney

All adversity I've had in my life, all my troubles and obstacles, have strengthened me. You may not realize it when it happens, but a kick in the teeth may be the best thing in the world for you.

~ Walt Disney

Benjamin Franklin's escape to New York did not go the way he planned. He traveled to the city with no specific employment plans, little money but a lot of hope. "I offered my services to the printer of the place, old Mr. Wm. Bradford," Franklin wrote in his autobiography. Bradford had no work for the young, transplanted printer. But Bradford had knowledge of the printing trade in Philadelphia, having gotten his start there until a disagreement with Pennsylvania's Governor Keith caused him to move north. More importantly, Bradford's son happened to be a printer in Philadelphia and his principal hand had recently died. The elder Bradford suggested Franklin try his luck there.

Young Ben pursued the opportunity. "Philadelphia was a hundred miles further. I set out, however, in a boat from Amboy, leaving my chest and things to follow me around by sea." Franklin's journey to Philadelphia was a bit of an adventure. The boat was met with a squall that tore its rotted sails to shreds and kept the craft from reaching the current that would have guided it to its destination. Instead, the boat was driven onto the Long Island shore but not before young Franklin plucked a drunken Dutchman who had fallen overboard out of the drink. The cold water sobered the man, who before drifting off to sleep asked Franklin to dry a book he had removed from his soaked pocket. Ever the craftsman, Franklin observed,

> It happened to be my old favourite author Bunyan's *Pilgrim's Progress* in Dutch, finely printed on good paper with copper cuts, a dress better than I had ever seen it wear in its own language.

The next leg of Franklin's trip was on foot. He traveled fifty miles to Burlington, where a boat could be boarded for the last leg of the journey. He found lodging with a kindly old woman in Burlington until the expected boat was to arrive. Franklin's scheduled departure was advanced when by chance he came upon a boat while walking along the riverbank one evening. The craft was packed with several passengers bound for Philadelphia, but the captain took Franklin aboard nonetheless. There was no wind to aid the passage and the broad-shouldered Franklin rowed all the way until nighttime navigating slowed the craft to a stop. The captain and passengers were not certain whether they had passed the city or not. In the morning they determined they still had a short distance to go, finally landing at the Market Street dock about eight or nine o'clock on a Sunday morning.

Franklin's first steps in the city where he decided to begin a career untethered to his brother were inauspicious. He cut quite the figure and made sure to describe his

6 | The Early Trials and Tribulations of Franklin and Disney

ragged look in his autobiography. It was a good way to demonstrate just how far he had come in life by the time he began to record the doings of his life in 1771. Franklin was not a stranger to vanity and the whole concept of humility would be something he spent a good deal of time reflecting on late in life.

That Sunday morning in 1723 represented a starting point of Franklin's solo act; he took care to describe himself at that juncture in his autobiography:

> I have been the more particular in this description of my journey, and shall be so of my first entry into that city, that you may in your mind compare such unlikely beginnings with the figure I have since made there. I was in my working dress, my best clothes being to come round by sea. I was dirty from my journey; my pockets were stuffed out with shirts and stockings; I knew no soul, nor where to look for lodging. Fatigued with walking, rowing, and want of sleep, I was very hungry, and my whole stock of cash consisted of a Dutch dollar and about a shilling in copper coin, which I gave to the boatman for my passage. At first they refused it on account of my having rowed, but I insisted on their taking it. A man is sometimes more generous when he has little money than when he has plenty, perhaps through fear of being thought to have but little.

Franklin's appetite led him to a bakery where he obtained some bread. Once there and being unfamiliar with various appellations of bread offered in his new city, he simply purchased "three pennyworth on any sort." Surprised by the quantity he received; Franklin went back to the street with one large roll under each arm as he ate a third. And in this extremis of poor dress and an overstock of bread, his future wife Deborah Read, then eighteen years old, first spied him.

The young man from Boston found work in a number of printing shops in his new city. The first two printers he was associated with, Bradford's son and another man named Keimer, provided less than promising opportunities for Franklin. According to Ben, "These two printers I found poorly qualified. Bradford had not been bred to it and was very illiterate, and Keimer, though something of a scholar, was a mere compositor, knowing nothing of presswork."

While the printing trade didn't hold initial promise for Franklin, a few circumstances developed that would have an impact on his future. The first was his choice of lodging. Having cleaned himself up from the first day in the city and having an opportunity to display a pleasing demeanor, he was able to take up boarding with young Deborah Read's mother. Keimer, Franklin's second employer, arranged it because Franklin's first landlord was Bradford. Bradford didn't want his tenant working for a competitor and Keimer did not have suitable lodgings available. The day would come when Ms. Read would become Ben's common-law wife but that was still years off.

The second circumstance involved the Pennsylvania governor, who became another character in the young man's pragmatic course of education. Though Franklin did his best to keep his Boston roots confidential, enough of the story of his origins eventually leaked out. Soon Franklin's brother-in-law Robert Holmes, who was master of a ship operated between Boston and Delaware, knew of Ben's whereabouts.

6 | The Early Trials and Tribulations of Franklin and Disney

> He (Holmes) being at New Castle, forty miles below Philadelphia, heard there of me and wrote me a letter mentioning the concern of my relations and friends in Boston at my abrupt departure, assuring me of their goodwill to me, and that every thing would be accommodated to my mind if I would return, to which he exhorted me very earnestly. I wrote an answer to his letter, thanked him for his advice, but stated my reasons for quitting Boston so fully and in such a light as to convince him that I was not so much in the wrong as he had apprehended.

Holmes happened to be in the company of Governor Keith when he received Franklin's response to his letter. Holmes shared the contents with the governor, who developed a fast appreciation for young Franklin's adroit use of language. Franklin soon developed a relationship with the governor. He even received a letter from his excellency recommending that Franklin should be set up in Philadelphia to make his fortune. Franklin took the governor's correspondence to Boston to ease a reunion visit with family he had left seven months before.

In late 1724, Governor Keith sent Franklin to London to purchase the printing equipment necessary to set up Franklin's own printing shop in Philadelphia, seemingly making good on his desire that Franklin should be set up as a tradesman. Governor Keith promised to send a letter of credit to London that would underwrite the entire venture. When Franklin arrived in London on December 24, 1724, there was no letter of credit, no financial assistance and no means to buy the printing equipment he would need to set up his own shop. Keith went back on his word and Franklin was stranded in

London where he would have to work and save his way back to Philadelphia.

During a year and a half in London, Ben got a crash course in frugality and credibility while he labored for two prestigious London printers, Samuel Palmer and James Watts. He worked hard, even observing how much more productive he became by drinking only water during the work day rather than beer, which the other tradesmen freely imbibed all day long. Franklin quickly realized that their productivity declined as their state of sobriety lessened once the day wore on. It was a lesson he would not soon forget. Frugality and efficiency in the workplace were lessons that would soon be the hallmarks of his success, but that success didn't come without early life lessons.

Walt Disney's path to success was not without early trials and tribulations as well. Walt's artistic talent was first honed by classes he took at the Kansas City Art Institute while still a teen and cartoons he drew for the McKinley High School newspaper. Walt continued creating illustrations while he was a driver for the ambulance corps during the war. While on duty in France he drew cartoons on the side of his ambulance and had some of his work published in the Army's newspaper, *Stars and Stripes*.

When Walt returned from France he took a job as an apprentice artist at the Pesmen-Rubin Commercial Art Studio. Perhaps the most consequential of Walt's experiences at the studio, which produced commercial advertising illustrations, was meeting fellow artist Ub Iwerks there. It was the beginning of an all-important creative relationship, though it would take some time before the full value of the combination would be realized.

6 | The Early Trials and Tribulations of Franklin and Disney

Once the advertising rush of the 1919 Christmas season had passed, Pesmen-Rubin laid off both Walt and Iwerks.

The newly unemployed artists formed the Iwerks-Disney Commercial Artists Company but the new venture couldn't generate enough revenue to support both of the partners. It was decided that Disney would leave and take a job with the Kansas City Film Ad Company while Iwerks built the partnership up enough to support them both. The plan soon failed and Iwerks went to work for the Kansas City Film Ad Company as well.

While working at the Film Ad Company, Disney's interest in animation deepened. He was a student of the cel (short for "celluloid") animation method, favoring it over the cutout method that some early animators were then using. His boss at the Film Ad Company didn't agree and Disney began producing shorts on his own with a coworker named Fred Harman. Walt worked feverishly to make the side business work, but in the end, as Harman quipped, "We just couldn't swing it."

Walt was not discouraged. He began to ponder the idea of leaving the Film Ad Company. Elias Disney, who had plenty of experience in business failings, discouraged his son from setting off on his own. He warned Walt that he could end up broke, but Walt's mind was made up. On May 18, 1921, he filed certificate of incorporation #39844 with the Missouri Secretary of State, forming Laugh-O-Gram Films, Inc. Walt was the new company's president. This was done despite the fact the law forbade him to serve as a company officer because he was not yet of legal age. The impetuous young executive had launched a firm purposed to "own, make, produce, buy, lease, rent, sell, release, distribute and deal in screen, industrial and commercial advertising and motion pictures of every kind and character."

Enlightenment & Enchantment

In many ways, some of the brashness of the new executive was tempered when, owing to a variety of circumstances, Walt found himself alone in Kansas City. His family, for various reasons, had left town. His brother Roy needed to move to a warmer climate to convalesce from tuberculosis. Then another brother, Herb, got a post office transfer to the milder climate of Oregon and his parents had grown just plain tired of Kansas City.

Walt was short on family support in Kansas City and his company assets were not in strong supply either. Laugh-O-Gram Films consisted of $3,000 worth of intellectual property and $1,500 of equipment. Attracting either investors or distributors for the content Walt was able to produce was a significant challenge. The company's finances tightened in 1922 and by the end of the year, Walt was living in his office and taking a bath once a week at Union Station. Walt was undercapitalized, stung by clients who defaulted on their obligations and operating in a place that could never be described as ideal for the film industry business.

When things became most dire, Walt got a bit of a lifeline thrown his way. He was rescued, at least momentarily. Walt was hired to make what today we would call a public service announcement (PSA). The job involved producing an educational film for a Kansas City dentist named Thomas B. McCrum. The film, *Tommy Tucker's Tooth,* featured two boys: Jimmie Jones, who had bad dental hygiene, and Tommy Tucker, who took care of his teeth. Both boys were looking for a job but only Tommy was able to land one as a result of his well-cared-for pearly whites. For his efforts to instill good dental habits, Walt was paid $500. It was too little, too late.

In July 1923, Laugh-O-Gram Films declared bankruptcy. Despite the end of the company, Walt was

6 | The Early Trials and Tribulations of Franklin and Disney

neither defeated nor dejected. He remained optimistic and his bankruptcy attorney Phineas Rosenberg observed, "Most people who file bankruptcy are disturbed or bitter." According to Rosenberg, "Walt wasn't."

Walt didn't walk away from the experience completely empty-handed. Near the end of the Laugh-O-Gram days, Walt had conceived a somewhat novel form of animation. It would be something he would resort to in his future films, even after he had achieved much success. In 1923, a much more modest effort involved including a live little girl in a world of animation. Walt called the short *Alice's Wonderland*. The concept was a further adaptation of an idea first hatched by Max and David Fleischer, established New York animators. The Fleischers' *Out of the Inkwell* short features cartoon figures who enters the real would, just the opposite of what Walt was creating when Laugh-O-Gram finally hit the skids. Though the film couldn't save him in Kansas City, *Alice's Wonderland* wasn't gone forever. It would be an idea that Walt was far from giving up on.

Walt's uncle Robert and his brother Roy both counseled Walt to get out of Kansas City after the bankruptcy was filed. Walt sold his cameras and used the proceeds to purchase a one-way ticket to Hollywood. Kansas City was not without lessons or experiences, though. One of his experiences, seemingly without any real future consequence at the time, would lie dormant for a few years. Years later Walt recounted it. The reminiscence involved a mouse that entertained him during the long hours he toiled at his Laugh-O-Gram desk.

> They used to fight for crumbs in my waste-basket when I worked alone late at night. I lifted them out and kept them in wire cages on my desk. I grew particularly fond of one brown house mouse.

He was a timid little guy. By tapping him on the nose with my pencil, I trained him to run inside a black circle I drew on my drawing board. When I left Kansas City to try my luck at Hollywood, I hated to leave him behind. So I carefully carried him to a backyard, making sure it was a nice neighborhood and the tame little fellow scampered to freedom.

That little brown mouse may have scampered to freedom when Walt left Kansas City but someday Walt would transform that little fellow into one of the world's most unforgettable characters.

Chapter 7

Franklin Takes a Wife

He that would thrive must ask his wife.

~ English Proverb

Benjamin Franklin left London on July 23, 1726. His trip home to Philadelphia was financed with the proceeds of a loan from Thomas Denham, a Philadelphia merchant. There were certain lures to Franklin's staying in Great Britain, despite the failure of Governor Keith's promises that had landed him there in the first place. It was Denham who persuaded Franklin to return to Pennsylvania. Denham was in London purchasing stock in trade for his import shop specializing in the sale of clothing and hardware. Denham proposed to hire Franklin as a bookkeeper and clerk to attend his store. Denham further suggested that in time there was the prospect of a promotion that would put Franklin in charge of establishing trading partners in the West Indies.

Franklin and Denham sailed from Gravesend on a warm summer day as Franklin would later write in his autobiography:

> Thus I passed about eighteen months in London. Most or part of the time, I worked hard at my business, and spent but little upon myself except in seeing plays and on books. My friend Ralph

had kept me poor. He owed my about twenty-seven pounds, which I was now never likely to receive. A great sum out of my small earnings. I loved him notwithstanding, for he had many amicable qualities. I had improved my knowledge, however, though I had by no means improved my fortune. But I had made some very ingenious acquaintances, whose conversation was of great advantage to me, and I had read considerably.

An Atlantic crossing in the eighteenth century took about twelve weeks, plenty of solitary time for a young man to ponder his future, to replay dreams, and more practically plot a course. Franklin wrote:

For the incidents of the voyage, I refer you to my journal where you will find them all minutely related. Perhaps the most important part of that journal is the *Plan* to be found in it, which I formed at sea, for regulating the future conduct of my life. It is the more remarkable as being formed when I was young and yet being pretty faithfully adhered to quite thro' to old age.

The shopkeeper and his new clerk landed in Philadelphia on October 11. Mr. Denham opened his store on Wall Street and Franklin "attended the business diligently, studied accounts, and grew in a little time expert at selling." The two lodged together and Denham, to quote Franklin, "counseled me as a father, having sincere regard for me." The amicable arrangement took a blow when in February 1727 both owner and clerk took ill, Franklin with pleurisy and Denham with some kind of distemper that Franklin had forgotten by the time he recorded the events in his autobiography. Franklin

7 | *Franklin Takes a Wife*

observed that his own malady nearly carried him off, but Denham was not as fortunate. Denham left his young clerk a small legacy in his will, as Franklin said, "(was a) a token of his kindness for me."

The shopkeeping business was not entirely agreeable to Franklin, and it is unlikely he would have returned to it after his illness had Denham survived as well. Franklin's options after Denham's death were not abundant. His old boss, Keimer, wanted him back, tempting him with the promise of "large wages." Keimer wanted Franklin to manage his printing business while Keimer gave his primary attention to the stationery shop he maintained. Franklin was reluctant to take Keimer up on his offer, having heard disparaging comments about Keimer while he was in London. To make matters worse, some of the unflattering commentary originated with Keimer's own wife. But Franklin was not successful in finding another shop to employ him and at last he "closed again with Keimer."

It didn't take Franklin very long to understand what prompted Keimer to pay him a generous wage. His boss's shop employed five other hands, including Hugh Meredith, a Welshman who, according to Franklin, "was honest and sensible, a man of experience and fond of reading but addicted to drinking." None of the men were particularly skilled or suited to the work they were assigned, whether it was compositing, pressing or bookbinding, and none were well paid. Keimer's design was to have Franklin train them and put his shop in order. Once that was accomplished, Franklin and his large wage would become quite dispensable.

As things progressed and Keimer's men developed experience, Franklin became less and less important to his employer. Finally, a small flap escalated to a bigger one and Franklin left the shop not intending to return. It was Meredith who persuaded Franklin to return long enough to hatch a plan. Meredith would persuade his father to purchase the necessary printing equipment in London to enable Franklin and Meredith to form a partnership. Franklin's contribution was his experience in exchange for the Meredith capital. The senior Meredith had no reservations about the arrangement. According to Ben, "his father was in town and approved of it—the more as he saw I had great influence with his son, had prevailed on him to abstain long from dram drinking, and he hoped might break him of that wretched habit entirely, when we came to be so closely connected."

In the last months of 1727, Franklin and Meredith bided their time while they secretly waited for their printing equipment to arrive from London. During this period Franklin helped Keimer execute a contract to print currency for the Colony of New Jersey. Franklin became an expert at it. The pace of Franklin's advancement began to transcend the world of the printing trade when he helped establish the Junto Club at this time. This society of young men, also referred to as the Leather Apron Club, met on Friday evenings to network, in modern parlance. At their meetings they worked on self-improvement, studied, and developed patterns of mutual aid and collaboration.

The year 1728, exactly two centuries before Walt Disney would make cutting-edge advances in animation and entertainment, commenced a period of four years that would firmly establish Benjamin Franklin. In his autobiography, Franklin took pains to explain his religious and moral development and philosophy as he embarked as a principal in the business world. After

7 | Franklin Takes a Wife

noting the difference between theories and real-world practice, he resolved that "truth, sincerity and integrity in dealings between man and man were of the utmost importance to the felicity of life, and I formed written resolutions (which still remain in my journal book) to practice them ever while I lived."

Part of Franklin's self-examination before beginning his partnership with Meredith was his treatment of Deborah Read, who he had courted before his time in London. While he was in the British capital, Deborah had married John Rogers when her correspondence to Franklin went ignored and his promise to return to Philadelphia after a few months did not materialize. Read's marriage to Rogers did not go well. Before Franklin completed his first year in business, Rogers stole a slave and abandoned both his wife and Philadelphia. Deborah Read must have weighed heavily on Franklin's mind for another reason in mid-1728. He fathered an illegitimate child sometime in late 1727 or early 1728. While some speculate, history has not revealed the child's mother. The affair was only the beginning of a number of revelations about Franklin's character that his son's life would reveal.

In the span of less than four years Franklin would purchase the *Pennsylvania Gazette* from Keimer, get himself elected as the official printer for Pennsylvania, and commence printing America's first German-language newspaper, *Philadelphische Zeitung.* He also drew up articles of agreement for the Library Company, an association that was "the first library in America," and perhaps most importantly, published the first edition of *Poor Richard's Almanac.*

Franklin's rapid advance in these years was not without trial and tribulation, most of which was the

Enlightenment & Enchantment

product of his partnership with Hugh Meredith. Actually, both Merediths, Franklin's partner and his father, were causing difficulties for the business, the younger Meredith by his unabated drinking and the senior for not following through on the final payment for the printing press and letters. Though repossession of the equipment was threatened by the creditor and Franklin had friends ready to rescue him financially, he was reluctant to abandon the Merediths as long as there was a chance the monies would ultimately be satisfied by the elder Meredith. At last, in 1730, Franklin offered to withdraw from the partnership thinking Meredith's father might be more inclined to complete his investment if his son was the sole proprietor. In the end Hugh Meredith faced reality and offered to solve his partner's problem.

> "No," says he, "my father has really been disappointed and is really unable; and I am unwilling to distress him further. I see this a business I am not fit for. I was bred a farmer, and it was a folly in me to come to town and put myself at thirty years of age an apprentice to learn a new trade. Many of our Welsh people are going to settle in North Carolina, where land is cheap. I am inclined to go with them and follow my old employment. You may find friends to assist you. If you will take the debts of the company upon you, return to my father the one hundred pounds he has advanced, pay my little personal debts, and give me thirty pounds and a new saddle, I will relinquish the partnership and leave the whole in your hands."

While Franklin ended one partnership in 1730, he entered another. Though the new one was not purely

7 | Franklin Takes a Wife

business, it lacked the romantic intensity to minimize some of the more pragmatic aspects of the union between Deborah Read and Benjamin Franklin. Franklin quipped he was lucky to have "one (wife) as much disposed to industry and frugality as myself." Franklin's ultimate union with Read was a way to correct what he deemed one of the great errata of his life. Read would raise Franklin's illegitimate son William and bear him two more children: Francis Folger Franklin on October 20, 1732, and Sarah Franklin on September 11, 1743. Franklin took Read as a common-law wife on September 1, 1730. In his autobiography, he explained the history of his relationship with Deborah and why their marriage was not a ceremonial or legal marriage.

> A friendly correspondence as neighbours and old acquaintances had continued between me and Miss Read's family, who all had a regard for me from the time of my first lodging in their house. I was often invited there and consulted in their affairs, wherein I sometimes was of service. I pitied poor Ms. Read's unfortunate situation, who was generally dejected, seldom cheerful, and avoided company. I considered my giddiness the cause of her unhappiness, tho' the mother was good enough to think the fault more her own than mine, as she had prevented our marrying in my absence. Our mutual affection was revived, but there were now great objections to our union. That match was indeed looked upon as invalid, a preceding wife being said to be living in England; but this could not easily be proved because of the distance. And tho' there was a report of his death, it was not certain. Then, tho' it should be true, he had left many debts which his successor might

be called upon to pay. We ventured, however, over all these difficulties, and I took her to wife, Sept. 1, 1730. None of the inconveniencies happened that we had apprehended; she proved a good and faithful helpmate, assisted me much by attending the shop; we throve together and ever mutually endeavoured to make each other happy. Thus I corrected that great erratum as well as I could.

In chronology, the last of the events marking this four-year epoch was Franklin's first publication of Poor Richard's Almanac on December 28, 1732. The almanac, written by Franklin under the pseudonym "Richard Saunders," helped set and cap the earliest years of Franklin's introduction to the worlds of business ownership and social activism. It many ways the almanac was a blend of for-profit business advice and a running public service advertisement complete with proverbs, practical household remedies, seasonal weather forecasts, and puzzles and other entertainments. The almanac was extremely popular throughout the colonies and sold quite well for its twenty-five-year run. Much of the wit Franklin included has become part of the American vernacular. Time-honored quotes from Franklin's almanac, for example, "Early to bed and early to rise, makes a man healthy, wealthy and wise" and "Work as if you were to live a hundred years, pray as if you were to die tomorrow" are still on the tip of people's tongues today. The cultural impact was wide and well recognized. The almanac brought Franklin much fame and created an image of the man as a folksy, wise and industrious achiever with a good sense of humor.

Franklin far exceeded his initial goal for Poor Richard's Almanac, to promote his printing business. He

7 | *Franklin Takes a Wife*

created a brand that helped support a lifetime of achievements. The future was bright and in typical Franklin fashion, sharing knowledge was not only desirable, but a way to advance his own objectives. He made the point in his own words as he took stock of his life in his autobiography.

In 1732 I first published my Almanac, under the name Richard Saunders; it was continued by me about twenty-five years, commonly called Poor Richard's Almanac. I endeavoured to make it both entertaining and useful, and it accordingly came to be in such demand that I reaped considerable profit from it, vending annually near ten thousand. And observing that it was generally read, scarce any neighbourhood in the province being without it, I considered it as a proper vehicle for conveying instruction among the common people, who bought scarce any other books. I therefore filled all the littles spaces that occurred between the remarkable days in the calendar with proverbial sentences, chiefly such as inculcated industry and frugality as the means of procuring wealth and thereby securing virtue..."

Chapter 8

Walt Goes West

One thing it takes to accomplish something is courage.

~ Walt Disney

Like Ben Franklin, Walt Disney's first marks on the world came after relocating. Both men made their move with few if any assets save for their desire to achieve, an ample amount of ingenuity and a deep optimism. In late July 1923, Walt stood on the platform at Kansas City's Union Station, not looking back, but instead holding a host of dreams for the future. His first-class ticket on the Santa Fe, California Limited belied his attire and accompanying luggage. Walt was wearing a borrowed suit. He later remembered, "I was in my pants and coat that didn't match, but I was riding first class." He was thin from a lack of regular nutrition and fortunately his brother Herbert's mother-in-law had prepared three packages of meals to sustain him on the train. His battered cardboard suitcase contained animation equipment and his most lavish adornment, a five-dollar pair of shoes.

If Walt's appearance was odd on his trip, there was no dampening of his spirit, only the promise of a new start. He may not have given any hint of that to his brother Roy, who upon his arrival in late February said,

"He looked like the devil. I remember he had a hacking cough and I used to tell him, 'For Christ sakes, don't you get TB.'"

Upon his arrival in California, Walt let a room from his uncle Robert Disney. Walt's goals at the time did not include cartoons or animation. The lure of movies and Hollywood was far stronger. Walt later recalled, "I was fed up with cartoons. My ambition at the time was to be a director." Disney set out seeking work at a Hollywood studio but there was no work in the offing. Though he talked his way onto a number of major studio lots and spent two months observing and canvassing for a position, he was not successful. His brother Roy advised him to get a job; Roy was selling vacuum cleaners door-to-door at the time. Walt had nothing of the sort in mind. Walt still had his *Alice's Wonderland* reel and searching for a distributor for the short and continuing with animation was a lot more attractive to him than knocking on doors to peddle consumer products. Uncle Robert came through once more when he allowed Walt to assemble a makeshift animation studio in his garage.

On August 25, 1923, Walt wrote to a successful cartoon distributor. Margaret Winkler was a rarity in a business dominated by men, but she was successful and represented some of the best in the business including Pat Sullivan of Felix the Cat fame and the Fleischer brothers. Walt first contacted Winkler while he was still in Kansas City. What he didn't know at that time was that Winkler was having trouble with both of her top-notch animators. Unfortunately for Walt he didn't have possession of the reel in May. The reel was in the possession of a Laugh-O-Gram creditor at that time. By August, however, Walt was not only in California, but he had possession of the reel. He sent to it Winkler, finally allaying her developing impatience for the film she was first prospected about three months before. Her response would be one of the most significant happenings in Walt Disney's early career.

On October 15, 1923, Winkler sent a telegram to Walt offering him a contract for twelve films. She proposed to pay $1,500 per film for the first six installments and $1,800 per film for the second set. Walt could not contain his excitement and went to share the news with his brother Roy, who was still in the veterans hospital recovering from his tuberculous infection. Walt needed Roy's help and begged him to leave the hospital. The very next day, Roy checked himself out of the hospital, never to return again. It was as if his brother's unbridled enthusiasm made being sick not an option for Roy. Walt signed the contract with Winkler the same day. While hurdles lay ahead, there was no turning back now. Walt and Roy would combine to establish a partnership that would last the entirety of their lives.

After some initial reluctance, the ever-helpful Uncle Robert loaned Walt $500 in late 1923 to help fund the new enterprise. It was not a foregone conclusion that Roy would be a part of the business. That was not his intention, especially given his utter lack of experience in anything to do with film or animation. The impetus of the business combination was simply Roy's desire to protect his younger brother. The Disney Brothers Cartoon Studio was born the same day Roy left the hospital and Walt signed the Winkler contract. The brothers not only became partners but roommates when Walt moved out of Uncle Robert's house to a room in the Oak Hill Apartments.

In December the brothers took a new apartment one block away from the studio. The Disney brothers' studio consisted of a room rented in the rear of a real estate firm and an adjacent outdoor lot. The brothers purchased a new camera, tools and supplies and got to work on the *Alice* shorts. Walt had to convince the family of the human star of the *Alice* shorts, Virginia Davis, to move from Missouri to California. It wasn't all that hard of a sell. Virginia's dad was a traveling furniture salesman who could operate as easily in California as in Missouri, and Virginia's mother was a stage mom with a deep interest in furthering her daughter's career in movies. Hollywood beckoned and the Davis family answered.

The series would be known as the *Alice Comedies* and Walt went to work on the first installment, doing all of the animation himself with his brother Roy operating the hand-cranked camera for the live-action scenes. The first short, *Alice's Day At Sea*, was finished in December 1923 and released in March 1924. In all, Disney would produce fifty-six *Alice Comedies*, the last of which was released in August 1927. There were a number of changes along the way.

A month after Walt signed the contract with Winkler, she married Charles Mintz. Winkler got pregnant and Mintz immediately took control of her company. The relationship with Mintz was far more difficult than the one with Winkler, whose criticism was always coupled with encouragement. Mintz's entry would foreshadow major future changes but for now, the parties coexisted for the benefit of the *Alice* series. The work associated with keeping up with the demands created by the series necessitated Walt increasing the Disney Brothers staff. Key additions, Ub Iwerks and Rollin "Ham" Hamilton, came in August 1924.

8 | Walt Goes West

Business wasn't the only thing the Disney brothers were establishing in the mid 1920s. In April 1925, Roy Disney married his longtime girlfriend Edna Francis, who he began dating in Kansas City about 1911. Roy's years in military service coupled with several years spent in hospitals recovering from tuberculosis had interrupted the course of their relationship. Walt fell in love too. Despite a pledge he wouldn't get married until he was age twenty-five, Walt married Lillian Bounds on July 13, 1925—a year and a half earlier than his target age and three months after his brother Roy's wedding.

Walt first met Lillian at his studio where she worked as an inker. At first there was no spark between Lillian and Walt, but that changed as the two got to know each other better during the rides home from work that Walt provided. The two were accompanied by a coworker who always got dropped off first. Soon Lillian began to see something in Walt: "I began to look at him like he was somebody," she recalled. Walt too developed an attraction and the free-wheeling entrepreneur committed to a domestic relationship just like his older brother had.

If the Disney weddings brought the new couples joy in the summer of 1925, the doings at the studio did nothing to dampen those buoyant feelings. The *Alice Comedies* were receiving good reviews and there was even talk about a book spin-off from the series. The partners were so confident in their future during the summer of 1925 that they put a $400 deposit on a piece of land with an office building on Hyperion Avenue in the Silver Lake district just east of Los Angeles. Long before the new Hyperion studio was up and running in the winter of 1926, relations with Mintz had soured'and this time the brothers had to deal with the dissatisfaction of the Davises, who were bridling against pay cuts that Walt was trying to impose to keep costs contained as his own profits were being squeezed by Mintz.

Despite the wrangling with Mintz, the brothers moved ahead with their new studio. When it finally opened, Walt had a conversation with Roy that would forever shape their company's brand. The way Roy told it, "One evening when Walt and I were discussing our move, Walt said to me, 'Roy, when we move to Hyperion, I'm going to have a large neon sign erected, reading 'Walt Disney Studios.' He looked at me as if expecting an argument. I said, 'If that's the way you want it.' And Walt said, 'That's the way I want it and that's the way it will be!' And that's the way it was." Forever more, the Disney Brothers Studio became Walt Disney Studios.

If the brothers' studio was gaining momentum, their *Alice Comedies* were not. The series began to lose steam and Walt knew it. Something new was needed to keep his young company competitive. Even before the last installment in the *Alice* series was produced, Walt turned his attention to a new character. Oswald the Lucky Rabbit was born. And if Oswald or his creator was lucky, it would take some time to fully see just how much so.

By March 1927, Mintz signed a contract with Universal, after the studio's ten-year absence from the world of animation, to produce twenty-six shorts based on Walt's sketches of his new rabbit character. Developed and tweaked, Oswald benefitted from the skillful animation of Disney's key employee Ub Iwerks. Walt, who didn't possess the artistic talent of Iwerks or his other animators had long before given up having a direct hand in that part of the business. Universal rejected the first film, and Walt and Iwerks went to work refining the character, making him younger and in Mintz's words, "more snappy looking." The refined Oswald took on a personality, something Walt believed was so important to the success of animated characters. With the panache and sass befitting the rabbit's personality, the series got off to a great start with the release of *Trolley Troubles* on September 5, 1927. By the end of the year, riding the success of Oswald, the number of Walt Disney Studios staff had risen to twenty-two. With Mintz, however, trouble was never far away.

The profits derived from the Oswald series enabled Walt and Roy to purchase adjoining lots of land on Lyric Avenue in the Silver Lake district in June. Soon after, the brothers built modest homes, by Hollywood standards, for their families at a total cost of $16,000. All of the progress and future promise came to an abrupt end in January 1928. Unbeknown to Walt, Mintz had been orchestrating a takeover of his company since as early as July the previous year. Mintz had attempted to lure disaffected staff away to create the Oswald series independent of Disney. Walt was shattered by the duplicity. Mintz signed a new three-year agreement with Universal to provide Oswald shorts on February 2, 1928, and Walt, still thinking he could save the relationship, went to New York three weeks later to negotiate a new and higher-priced agreement with his distributor. Disney was about to learn the lesson of his life.

There would be no negotiating a price increase for the Disney studio. In fact, Mintz's counterproposal was that he would take over the studio and pay Walt and Roy $200 per weeks as his employees. Walt refused and went to Universal, which fluffed him off. As Iwerks, who stayed loyal to Walt, warned from California, Mintz was luring away Disney's staff. If this wasn't a big enough problem, the next reality was a much more potent gut-punch. Walt learned his studio didn't own the rights to Oswald. That intellectual property belonged to Universal. Walt had no staff, no contract and no Oswald. And as odd as it might sound, it might have been the best thing that happened to him. Perhaps Oswald (or Walt) was lucky after all.

The train ride home was punctuated by either rage or, as Lillian would say, fear. It surely could have been both. Walt needed a new idea, and he needed one soon. Legend has it the idea of a mouse came from the tiny fellow Walt had trained in his last days at the Laugh-O-Gram office in Kansas City. Walt also said the idea of a mouse came to him on the train home, somewhere between Chicago and Los Angeles. Walt wrote a scenario about a mouse who wanted to impress his mouse girlfriend by building and flying a plane across the Atlantic. His character in *Plane Crazy* was emulating and borrowing the fame of Charles Lindberg's history-making nonstop flight from New York to Paris in May 1927.

As legend has it, Walt's original moniker for his mouse was Mortimer. When his wife Lillian registered her dislike, she suggested the name Mickey. And though Iwerks once corroborated the naming process, he later retracted his statement. Lillian herself was not committed about where the name came from. However, the famous mouse got his name, it would soon become one of the most recognizable characters and brands in the history of the world, but not before Walt could sell his Mickey Mouse films.

The path ahead for the marketing of the mouse would not be an easy one. In time, and out of his own frustration, Walt decided to remake his Mickey Mouse films with sound, something that was in its infancy in 1928. Walt went to New York on May 4, 1928, earnestly looking to find a distributor for his four Mickey Mouse films. Over the next two months, Walt lugged his reels from distributor to distributor. Each time the story was the same. There was a screening and a polite "we will be in touch if interested."

Walt was running low on finances, and even worse, his confidence was starting to erode too. It may have been the darkest hour. The Disneys had mortgaged their homes and tapped every avenue, even selling Walt's prized Moon Roadster automobile, to float the studio's expenses, the sound technology, and Walt's extended trip. With little time or money to spare, a ray of light finally appeared.

Harry Reichenbach was the manager of the Colony Theater on Broadway. He had experience representing film companies. Per chance he happened to witness one of the screenings Walt ran for a prospective distributor. He liked the film enough to approach Walt and offered him $500 for a two-week run at the Colony. Walt worried that the plan might jeopardize his chances of landing a distributor. Reichenbach told him the distributors only understood how good a film was after the public voiced its response. Though in no position to bargain, Walt countered with a $1,000 offer and Reichenbach agreed.

Steamboat Willie debuted at the Colony on November 18, 1928—Mickey Mouse was born. Walt attended every showing of the film, nervously at first, anticipating the audience response. The audience reception was remarkably favorable and the reviews just as good. Walt Disney had a genuine phenomenon on his hands. Six minutes of film with sound, not the first to use sound, but the best to adapt the new technology, changed everything. Walt and his company changed animation, changed entertainment, paired a brand with marketing like no one ever had and laid a solid cornerstone for a company that would eventually become the greatest entertainment empire in the history of the planet.

Both Benjamin Franklin and Walt Disney had significant successes before they were age thirty. For most, triumphs like Franklin's *Poor Richard's Almanac* and Disney's Mickey Mouse would be the singular achievement by which their entire careers would be judged. Franklin and Disney, both twenty-six years old when their respective milestones were reached, were just beginning. Energetic and filled with optimism, decades of accomplishment lay ahead. Their impact on America, not fully understood in their earliest years, was nevertheless taking on a definite shape and their contemporaries and generations to come would notice.

Chapter 9

Success Visits Again

Without continual growth and progress, such words as improvement, achievement and success have no meaning.

~ B. Franklin

Most highly successful people are known for a singular achievement. They have a clear pinnacle, a transcendent moment that will forever define their legacy. Rare is the celebrated citizen who is noteworthy for multiple exploits that have changed history and the world around them. Benjamin Franklin and Walt Disney enjoy the distinction of being among the few in this category. Each man lived a life filled with a multitude of accomplishments that changed their world and the world of generations to come.

It wasn't in the twilight of their lives that either Walt Disney or Ben Franklin followed their first successes with new ones. Both pursued their future with an energy that rarely waned and never extinguished. And both were far from finished in displaying their creative genius for the world to see after their first major triumphs. Somehow, they were able to fully understand human needs and find ways to make life just a little better.

Enlightenment & Enchantment

By the time he was thirty-six years old, Benjamin Franklin the inventor was devising a better way to keep people warm in their homes. With the exception of sustenance, one can hardly conceive of a more basic human need than a temperate habitation. Before 1742, American colonists heated their homes with open fireplaces. While a long tradition in home heating, an open hearth was not the most efficient way to warm living space, as Franklin observed. Franklin invented a new way to heat a home. The Franklin stove, as his innovation became known, stood in the center of a room. Constructed of cast iron, the transfer of heat from the wood fire radiated heat, even after the fire was spent. The rear of the stove was constructed with baffles to improve the airflow through the stove, efficiently conducting heat throughout the room. Not only was the heating more effective, but it was also far more efficient, consuming much less wood than a traditional fireplace.

The Franklin stove greatly improved the quality of life in colonial America. In his autobiography, Franklin recorded not only the invention but a philosophy he would attach to other life-changing inventions he conceived later in life.

> In Order of Time I should have mentioned before, that having in 1742 invented an open Stove, for the better warming of Rooms and at the same time saving Fuel, as the fresh Air admitted was warmed in Entring, I made a Present of the Model to Mr. Robert Grace, one of my early Friends, who having an Iron Furnace, found the Casting of the Plates for these Stoves a profitable Thing, as they were growing in demand. To promote that Demand I wrote and published a Pamphlet Intitled, *An account of the New-Invented*

9 | Success Visits Again

pennsylvania fire places: Wherein their Construction and manner of Operation is particularly explained; their Advantages above every other Method of warming Rooms demonstrated; and all Objections that have been raised against the Use of them answered and obviated, &c. This Pamphlet had a good Effect, Govr. Thomas was so pleas'd with the Construction of this Stove, as describ'd in it that he offer'd to give me a Patent for the sole Vending of them for a Term of Years; but I declin'd it from a Principle which has ever weigh'd with me on such Occasions, viz. *That as we enjoy great Advantages from the Inventions of others, we should be glad of an Opportunity to serve others by any Invention of ours, and this we should do freely and generously.* An Ironmonger in London, however, after assuming a good deal of my Pamphlet, and working it up into his own, and making some small Changes in the Machine, which rather hurt its Operation, got a Patent for it there, and made as I was told a little Fortune by it. And this is not the only Instance of Patents taken out for my Inventions by others, tho' not always with the same Success; which I never contested, as having no Desire of profiting by Patents my self, and hating Disputes. The Use of these Fireplaces in very many Houses both of this and the neighboring Colonies, has been and is a great Saving of Wood to the Inhabitants.

In a rather uncanny parallel, Walt Disney's second major success, like Franklin's, came at age twenty-six as well. Walt's second major invention, one that changed both animation and the motion picture industry, did not come without much effort. It took nearly four years to complete and it all began in the winter of 1934.

One of Disney's animators, Ken Anderson, recalled the evening the story of *Snow White and the Seven Dwarfs* was introduced. According to Anderson, Walt gathered a group of employees one afternoon and gave them all fifty cents to pay for their dinner at a restaurant across the street from the studio. He further requested they all return after their evening repast to the studio's soundstage. The group convened back at the studio about 7:30 p.m.

About fifty studio employees took their seats on the tiered wooden benches. Walt, standing on a darkened stage lit by a single spotlight, had their full attention. He informed the assembled he was going to produce an animated feature film. Walt, there and then, acted out the story of *Snow White and the Seven Dwarfs,* character by character. He interpreted Snow White, the queen, the prince and each of the dwarfs, taking care to bring all to life with great fullness and character. Animator Joe Grant said that Walt was "a spellbinder." Anderson added, "(W)e were carried away." Walt held their attention for the three hours it took to complete his full performance.

The group that left the soundstage was filled with enthusiasm. Walt had sold his people on the idea of an animated feature. He had succeeded in sharing his vision. A feature-length animation would not be completed without great attention to detail and lots of arduous work. The staff buy-in would be critical to the completion of the project. There would be many times ahead that the staff would have to draw on the energy created by Walt's performance on the studio soundstage that winter evening in 1934.

Not only would *Snow White* be feature length, but it represented a departure from shorts highly dependent on gags in favor of a narrative drama. The challenge was

9 | Success Visits Again

not limited to the demands of immeasurable animation but also a coherent and engaging story. Walt attracted and recruited scores of new animators at the height of the Depression while Roy fretted just how to finance the whole endeavor. Walt brought in animals and life models to hone the animators' craft. By mid-1938, the Disney studio would employ five hundred people, all part of a team dedicated to Walt's objective, all filled with a spirit born of Walt's vision.

The rough animation of *Snow White* was completed in December of 1936, one year before the date of the movie's eventual release. The details were of the utmost importance to Walt, from the realism of the colors to the fine points of the character animation. The film incorporated another level of realism utilizing a multi-plane camera system developed by the Disney studio. The new camera system added depth to the film by adjusting backgrounds in relation to the animated figures as in real life, with each plane's camera picking up one of the layers that made up the whole scene.

As work on the film progressed, the deadline of Christmas 1937 became both daunting and a constant source of pressure as the hours and days ticked away. The staff worked twenty-four-hour days in eight-hour shifts. All hands were on deck while Roy scampered to feed the all-consuming beast with more and more money. Fortunately for Walt, representatives of his distributor, RKO Radio Pictures, sat for a screening of a small portion of the film in September 1937. They were favorably impressed and were confident that the undertaking would be a profitable one.

Snow White premiered on December 21, 1937, at the Carthay Circle Theatre in Los Angles. It was an immediate box office and critical success. Frank Nugent's review in *The New York Times* noted the film was as important as, "*The Birth of the Nation* or the birth of Mickey Mouse." *Snow White* earned $8 million dollars in its initial release against a production cost of $1.5 million. It became the highest-selling animated film in history and one of the highest grossing of any genre. The film was something the Motion Picture Academy didn't quite know how to deal with. It received a nomination for best musical score in 1938 and an honorary Oscar in 1939, uniquely consisting of one regular-sized statuette and seven miniature ones presented by Shirley Temple. In 1989 the Library of Congress deemed *Snow White* "culturally, historically, or aesthetically important" as one of the first twenty-five films selected for preservation in the National Film Registry.

Beyond all the accolades, including Walt being conferred honorary doctorate degrees by Harvard and Yale on successive days in June 1938, *Snow White* transformed the motion picture industry, animation, and our culture. Born solely from a blank surface and Walt's imagination, an entirely new art form arose: feature-length animation. Audiences were no longer limited to seeing short cartoons, cute or funny in nature. Walt extended animation to dramatic, adult themes that could make one laugh, hope, identify, and yes, cry. It was truly groundbreaking like few things are in the entertainment mediums. At age thirty-one, Walt Disney had achieved his second stunning success. He wasn't finished yet and America still had much in store from the creative genius of the man who dared to dream.

Chapter 10

Electricity Propels Franklin's Stature

Before I proceed in relating the part I had in public affairs...it may not be amiss here to give some account of the rise and progress of my philosophical reputation.

~ Benjamin Franklin

Franklin lived during the Enlightenment, or age of reason, when science or natural philosophy began to displace faith-based social authority. The philosophical reputation Franklin writes about in his autobiography is in fact natural philosophy or the scientific study of the world around him. Like Walt Disney, Benjamin Franklin was far from finished after his initial stunning successes. If Walt had Mickey Mouse and *Snow White,* Ben had an almanac that in the colonies sold second only to the Bible and a stove that revolutionized home heating. Though they lived in far different worlds, both men's stores of dynamic energy and unquenchable imagination continued unabated.

Franklin spent part of his fortieth year visiting Boston. While in the city of his birth, Franklin became acquainted with Dr. Spence, who had recently arrived from Scotland. Dr. Spence demonstrated electrical experiments to Franklin. Though the demonstration was, according to Franklin, "imperfectly performed, as he (Spence) was not very expert," Franklin was hooked. In the aftermath of the display, he noted, "but being on a subject quite new to me, they equally surprised and pleased me."

Dr. Spence's experiments were performed with a Leyden jar, named for the Dutch university where its inventor taught. The jar was a primitive capacitor capable of temporarily storing and discharging an electrical charge quickly. Soon after Franklin returned to Philadelphia, and with the electrical experiments fresh on his mind, he received a package from London. The sender, Peter Collinson of London's Royal Society, had sent a glass tube to be used for, coincidentally, electrical experimentation. Franklin had previously corresponded with Collinson and the glass tube that arrived in Philadelphia in 1746 would give rise to several communications between Franklin and Collinson. Franklin made immediate use of the gift from Collinson.

> Soon after my return to Philadelphia, our library company received from Mr. Peter Collinson, F.R.S., of London, a present of a glass tube, with some account of the use of it in making such experiments. I early seized the opportunity of repeating what I had seen in Boston, and by much practice acquired great readiness in performing those also which we had an account of from England, adding a number of new ones. I say much practice, for my house was continually full for some time with people who came to see these new wonders. To divide a little this incumbrance among my friends, I caused a number of similar tubes to be blown at our glass

house, with which they furnished themselves, so that we had at length several performers. Among these the principal was Mr. Kinnersley, an ingenious neighbor, who, being out of business, I encouraged to undertake showing the experiments for money, and drew up for him two lectures in which the experiments were ranged in such order and accompanied with explanations, in such method as that the foregoing should assist in comprehending the following. He procured an elegant apparatus for the purpose, in which all the little machines that I had roughly made for myself nicely formed by instrument makers. His lectures were well attended and gave great satisfaction, and after some time he went thro' the Colonies exhibiting them in every capital town and picked up some money. In the West India Islands, indeed, it was with difficulty the experiments could be made, from the general moisture of the air.

Franklin's experiments ranged from fascinating to dangerously amusing. Early on, Franklin sent electrical shocks into the limbs of paralyzed individuals. He observed the impact, which in a number of the cases was of benefit to his "patient." He was centuries ahead of his time, though with Franklin's experiments the subjects' initial gains from the "treatment" soon disappeared. Other experiments were not as serious.

Just two days before Christmas Day in 1750, Franklin attempted to entertain his guests by killing a turkey with an electrical charge. On Christmas Day he wrote, "I have lately made an experiment in electricity that I desire never to repeat." Things did not go as planned. Unwittingly, Franklin found himself holding both a positive and negative charge. He recounted the accident: "Two nights ago, being about to kill a turkey by shock from two large glass jars, containing as much electrical fire as forty cannon phials, I inadvertently took the whole through my own arms and body, by receiving the fire from the united top wires with one hand, while the other hand held a chain connected with the outside of both jars." His audience heard a loud bang and saw a flash. Franklins experienced neither. The shock, which knocked him to the floor, deprived him of his senses. He later wrote, "The first thing I took notice of was a violent, quick shaking of my body which gradually remitting, my sense as gradually returned." Fortunately for the embarrassed scientist, the numbness and soreness passed after a few days. His interest in electricity was unabated though.

Parlor entertainments were one thing, but Franklin broke new ground with his bold theory that there was a "sameness of lightening with electricity." His idea was not well received. Franklin sent a paper on his theory to a Dr. Mitchell, an acquaintance and member of the London Royal Society. The members scoffed. "Dr. Mitchell wrote me word that it had been read but was laughed at by the connoisseurs." Not all was lost, however.

Franklin had sent a number of papers to Peter Collinson. The totality was shown to Dr. Fothergill who, accordingly to Franklin, "thought them of too much value to be stifled and advised the printing of them." Collinson gave the papers to a Mr. Cave who published *Gentleman's Magazine* for inclusion in his periodical. But Cave decided to print the papers as a pamphlet to which Dr. Fothergill wrote a preface. In his autobiography, Franklin revealed what happened next.

10 | Electricity Propels Franklin's Stature

> Cave, it seems, judged rightly for his profit; for by the additions that arrives afterwards, they swelled to a quarto volume, which has had five editions and cost him nothing for copy-money.

The book, *Experiments and Observations on Electricity Made at Philadelphia in America,* had little immediate impact in England. Before the volume caught on in London, a copy found its way to the other side of the English Channel. Count de Buffon, in Franklin's words, "a philosopher deservedly of great reputation in France and indeed all over Europe, 'prevailed with Mr. Dalibard to translate them into French, and they were printed at Paris.'"

Franklin's theory found quick criticism in France as well—there chiefly directed by "the Abbé Nollet, preceptor in natural philosophy to the Royal Family, and able experimenter." Nollet doubted not only Franklin's theory but also the existence of anyone named Franklin from the American colonies. Franklin briefly considered taking up his pen to debate Nollet but thought better of it. Conjecture across the ocean by two men who spoke different languages didn't seem like a profitable endeavor to the accomplished man from Philadelphia. Soon enough any need for discourse would end.

Franklin relates the wholesale shift to his way of thinking best.

> What gave my book the more sudden and general celebrity was the success of one of its proposed experiments made by Messrs. Dalibard and Delor at Marly for drawing lightning from the clouds. This encouraged the public attention everywhere.

M. Delor, who had an apparatus for experimental philosophy and lectured in that branch of science, undertook to repeat what he called the "Philadelphia Experiments," and after they were performed before the King and court, all the curious of Paris flocked to see them. I will not swell this narrative with an account of that capital experiment, nor of the infinite pleasure I received in the success of a similar one I made soon after with the kite at Philadelphia, as both are to be found in the histories of electricity.

The Dalibard experiment was conducted at Marly, a town near Paris on May 10, 1752. Dalibard constructed a high tower topped with a long iron rod. During a lightning storm a man held a metal wire near the end of the rod and observers saw sparks jump from the rod to the wire. Franklin's theory was proved, and in the process, he has forever been credited with the invention of the lighting rod. The invention solved a problem that had long plagued mankind, lighting-generated building fires.

Five months subsequent to the Dalibard experiment, Franklin conducted the more famous electrical experiment that has since created the indelible image of Franklin the scientist and electrical theorist. On October 19, 1762, Franklin published a statement about his experiment in his newspaper, the *Pennsylvania Gazette*. Apparently not having a high towner and long iron rod at the ready like Dalibard, (and recognizing the danger attendant to using the rod), Franklin adapted his experiment using the much-celebrated kite. He constructed the kite with two cedar strips and then stretched a silk handkerchief across them. The kite's tail was fashioned from two different materials. The upper section, closest to the kite,

10 | Electricity Propels Franklin's Stature

was made of hemp and the lower section was fabricated from silk. Near the bottom of the hemp section Franklin placed a metal key. While flying the kite in a storm, Franklin stood under the cover of a shed where the silk portion of the tail was kept dry. Soon Franklin noticed the hemp strands were standing on end as they became saturated with rain and developed an electrical charge from the ambient air of the storm. When Franklin placed his finger near the key he felt the spark as the positive and negative charges were coming together.

Franklin's kite experiment was read to the Royal Society on December 21 and the next year the Society would visit praise on the man most wholly discredited less than two years earlier. With justifiable pride, Franklin repeated the pointed reverence in the pages of his autobiography. Franklin was no longer an oddity from across the Atlantic but now a celebrated scientist with an international reputation, something afforded to just about no one ever from North America.

> Dr. Wright, an English physician then at Paris, wrote to a friend who was of the Royal Society an account of the high esteem my experiments were in among the learned abroad, and of their wonder that my writings had been so little noticed in England. The Society on this resumed the consideration of the letters that had been read to them, and the celebrated Dr. Watson drew up a summary account of them and of all I had afterwards sent to England on the subject, which he accompanied with some praise of the writer. This summary was then printed in London, particularly the very ingenious Mr. Canton, having verified the experiment of procuring lightning from the clouds by a pointed rod and

85

acquainting them with the success, they soon made me more than amends for the slight with which they had before treated me. Without my having made any application for that honour, they chose me a member and voted that I should be excused the customary payments, which would have amounted to twenty-five guineas, and ever since have given me their transactions gratis. They also presented me with the gold medal of Sir Godfrey Copley for the year 1753, the delivery of which was accompanied by a very handsome speech of the present, Lord Macclesfield, wherein I was highly honoured.

And so, Benjamin Franklin added to his retinue of accomplishments the title of natural philosopher. In Franklin's case, he was not only a celebrated natural philosopher but one whose bold theory had changed his world, in more ways than one. Franklin had not only advanced science but created for himself something no other American had yet achieved, a truly international reputation. Both would have immense consequences in time to come.

Chapter 11

Disney's Restless Mind Looks Ahead

All our dreams can come true, if we have the courage to pursue them.

~ Walt Disney

Before they reached their fiftieth annum, both Benjamin Franklin and Walt Disney had done a lot. The phenomenal success Walt enjoyed from *Snow White* was followed with a number of other feature-length animations, usually referred to as "The Big Five." In addition to *Snow White*, those movies are considered to also include *Pinocchio* (1940), *Fantasia* (1940), *Dumbo* (1941), and *Bambi* (1942). Each of these movies broke ground in some way. And while box office returns for the four succeeding films may not have reached the heights of *Snow White*, each film was a masterpiece of animation and story content in its own right. *Pinocchio* is still heralded for its animation and *Fantasia* for its cutting-edge inclusion of classical music conducted by Leopold Stokowski. *Bambi* represented additional strides in animation and realism while conveying a story filled with emotion, and *Dumbo* was no less dramatically complex. One critic praised *Dumbo* as "the highest achievement yet reached in the seven arts since the white man landed on the continent."

The four movies made in the wake of *Snow White* were all impacted by World War II, first in European theatres and later domestically. An article about *Dumbo* planned for *TIME's* December 29 issue was dropped as the cover story when the attack on Pearl Harbor changed the focus of the country. The war changed much more than magazine covers and declining box office revenue for Disney was further squeezed by a shrinking margin between sales and the growing costs associated with cutting-edge feature animation.

The studio's finances were not the only thing changed by the war, as five hundred US Army troops quickly set up an antiaircraft installation on the studio lot to protect the nearby Lockheed Aircraft factory. Walt made government training films to supplement the studio's diminished receipts and pivoted to less expensive projects, including nature documentaries and live-action films.

When the war was finally behind him, Disney returned to animation, but his first forays were with films that packaged together a number of subjects. The first was *Melody Times* released on May 27, 1948. The film included seven vignettes, two of which were the legend of Johnny Appleseed and the story of Texas hero Pecos Bill. A review appearing in the *Los Angeles Times* found those two segments "more endearing" than the rest. Generally, however, reviews were less than enthusiastic.

The following year Disney released *The Adventures of Ichabod and Mr. Toad,* a two-segment film based on two different sources, the short story "The Legend of Sleepy Hollow" (1820) by Washington Irving and the book *The Wind in the Willows* (1918) by British author Kenneth Grahame. Though the reviews were more favorable than those for *Melody Time,* Walt's interest in the studio's offerings had waned and his enthusiasm for its newest offering wasn't any more keen. In 1950, *Cinderella,* the

11 | Disney's Restless Mind Looks Ahead

studio's first feature-length animation since before the war, brought the studio back to its animation heyday, but just as importantly revived box office sales and profits that exceeded even the most optimistic estimates. The cash was sorely needed. Yet despite the glow of the film's critical praise and the much-needed financial infusion, Walt was less than impressed with the quality of the animation or the studio's efforts in general. Walt needed a new challenge. His creative sense yearned for something novel. Stunted, stifled, or simply bored, he needed a different purpose.

In another interesting parallel, both Walt Disney and Benjamin Franklin experienced marked life transitions as they approached or attained their fiftieth year of life. Franklin's life took a decided turn toward diplomacy and statecraft and Disney took up a decided interest in trains and small-town America. In many ways, Walt was retreating to the warmth of boyhood memories made during his days in Marceline. He was getting in touch with his inner child in the process. The new pursuits of Franklin and Disney would have a significant impact on the world in which they lived and for many years to come. Both men had achieved much, enough to fill multiple lifetimes, but there was still much more to come for both.

Disney's transformation came along innocently enough. During the summer of 1947, Walt began instinctively creating a path around the perimeter of his yard. It was solitary work by a man who kept to himself far more than the outside world might have thought. During that summer, it was especially so as he became increasingly disengaged from work at the studio. Lillian and others at the studio were aware of Walt's growing lack of interest in the doings at work.

Enlightenment & Enchantment

Hazel George knew Walt's innermost thoughts as well as anyone, maybe better than all. She was hired as the Disney studio's nurse and had previously received training in psychiatric nursing. She became Walt's closest confidant, someone he deeply trusted. She would visit Walt at five o'clock each day as the work day ended. The routine they established included a massage, as therapy for Walt's polo injury, a Scotch Mist, and conversation that was just as therapeutic for Walt as the massage. Such was the level of trust that George knew all too well that Walt needed some kind of emotional elixir to continue.

A crossroad came when George suggested Walt take in a railroad fair in Chicago in 1948. The fair celebrated the development of the railroad industry in America. George knew that trains held Walt's fascination, a throwback to the carefree days of his youth in Marceline. In fact, on December 8, 1947, Walt had written his sister Ruth, "I bought myself a birthday-Christmas present—something I wanted all my life—an electric train." Walt's doctor had told him he needed a hobby and the busy studio executive decided model trains was the perfect one. He was so enthusiastic about it he bought Lionel model train sets for three of his grandnephews as well.

Walt set his Lionel train up in the outer rooms adjoining his office. His new and elaborately displayed hobby was pretty apparent to the studio staff. Walt knew that animator Ward Kimball was a fellow train enthusiast who had built a full-scale railroad and nine hundred feet of narrow-gauge track in his San Gabriel yard in 1945. Another Disney animator, Ollie Johnston, was in the process of building a one-twelfth-scale steam train for a track in his backyard. Johnston took Walt to the Santa Monica machine shop where the locomotive was being

11 | Disney's Restless Mind Looks Ahead

built. Walt fell in love with it all, exclaiming, "By God, I want one of those for my own."

With that backdrop, Disney and Kimball boarded the Santa Fe Super Chief and headed to Chicago. The fair included the display of full-size trains traveling across a huge stage. One unforgettable display hit Walt hard. The impressive exhibit included the Lincoln funeral train drawn by a Civil War-era locomotive. One of the black-draped cars was from the original train. As the train was drawn across the stage slowly, an African American couple walked with it to the playing of "The Battle Hymn of the Republic." Each time he viewed the solemn reenactment, Walt's eyes filled with tears.

The excursion to Chicago was cathartic for Walt. On the way out, he spent two nights regaling Kimball with a recitation of his life history, over glasses of whiskey. "He was very preoccupied with his own history and spent two nights telling me his entire history," Kimball recalled, "from the time he was a boy, sold papers and the whole thing." The trip proved to be a step in a process, one that would have far-ranging impacts. Little that Walt did was without purpose.

When he returned from Chicago he began making plans for his own train. Walt had plans drawn based on a one-eighth scale of the Central Pacific engine, Number 173. The studio machine shop and machinist Roger Broggie, who had already taught Walt how to operate a lathe, were enlisted to help fabricate Walt's train. Suddenly the studio mogul was passing his days as an apprentice machinist and having the time of his life doing it. Finally, just before Christmas 1948, Walt's train was ready for a test run. Walt set up three hundred feet of track on the studio's soundstage to test his new pride and joy. The train worked well enough to be set up in the yard of his new home, something that didn't occur without some objection from Lillian. While she was happy about the relief her husband experienced from his new hobby, she wasn't quite ready to surrender the yard of the new home they were about to build.

The couple had found a suitable lot of land on Carolwood Drive in Holmby Hills, a residential area located near Beverly Hills. There they built a home for their family and the Carolwood Pacific railroad pulled by a locomotive named the Lilly Belle. Walt had his lawyer draft a "tongue-in-cheek" agreement as concerned the railroad, himself the "party of the first part," his wife "the party of the second party" and his minor daughters, Diane and Sharon, collectively "the parties of the third part."

> WHEREAS, Walt is or is about to become the sole proprietor and owner of a certain railroad company known as the Walt Disney R.R. Co., which railroad company proposes to construct and operate a railroad in, on, upon and over the right of way hereinafter described and delineated, in the operation of which railroad Walt desires to have and at all times to retain complete, full, undisturbed, unfettered and unrestricted control and supervision, unhampered and unimpeded by the other parties hereto or by any of them, they having heretofore made known and asserted to Walt in various sundry and devious ways their collective intention to reign supreme within, and so far as concerns, the aforesaid residence, and
>
> WHEREAS, the Second and Third Parties, in the future and notwithstanding Walt's ownership of the fee title to the aforesaid parcel of land, and

11 | Disney's Restless Mind Looks Ahead

notwithstanding their many enthusiastic assurances verbally given to Walt in their present enthusiasm over said new residence and their anticipated pleasures and happiness therein, may, and probably will, seek to assert rights, privileges and authorities inconsistent with Walt's reserved and retained control and supervision over said railroad company and the operation of said railroad company upon the right of way herein referred to, all to the detriment of said railroad and its efficient, profitable and pleasurable operation, and to the injury of Walt's peace of mind (the presence and soundness of which mind Second and Third Parties hereby admit).

THAT WHEREAS, Walt and Lillian are husband and wife and Diane and Sharon are their children, in which family there presently exists an atmosphere of love, understanding and trust which all parties hereto are intensely desirous of preserving;

NOW, THEREFORE, in consideration of the promises and of other good and valuable considerations the receipt of which is hereby acknowledged by Lillian, Diane and Sharon, the said Lillian, Diane and Sharon hereby jointly and severally quit claim, transfer, assign and set over to Walt all their right, title and interest in and to the right of way..."

Walt's merriment and sense of whimsy was not shared by all. Some industry watchers were downright bewildered. *The New York Times* film critic Bosley Crowther "came away sad" after watching a giant of American entertainment "wholly, almost wearily, concerned with the building of a miniature railroad engine and a string of cars in the workshops of the studio. All of his zest for invention for creating fantasies, seemed to be going into this plaything." What Crowther didn't know was that the inner workings of Disney's mind were anything but miniature in scale. According to Disney biographer Bob Thomas, "None of Walt Disney's endeavors, not even his hobbies, was without purpose, and the Carolwood-Pacific formed part of his growing plan for a new kind of enterprise for Walt Disney Productions." Before 1948 was done Walt was talking about plans for an eleven-acre plot the studio owned across the street on Riverside Drive. His ideas, reduced in a memo written on August 31 and titled "Mickey Movie Park," involved an informal park complete with a village green, a small town hall, a bandstand, and benches. Walt believed that amusement parks could be designed and built better, cleaner and with a greater level of entertainment for the whole family, including the adults. "Mickey Mouse Park" would recall a simpler time of small-town America with all of the shops of yore, including a candy store, soda fountain, hobby and book stores and the like, all anchored by a railroad station. Walt's imagination had taken flight once again. All that was left was the task of realizing his dreams once more.

Chapter 12

Franklin Pursues a New Vocation

Well Done is better than Well Said.

~ B. Franklin

Franklin's life, like Disney's, followed a different path during his fourth decade. In the case of the eldest Founding Father, the line of demarcation might have been more defined. Franklin was nominated to serve in the Pennsylvania Assembly during the summer of 1751. He was forty-five years old, almost the same age as Disney when the studio mogul began his fascination with trains. During his time in the printing trade, Franklin well understood that mixing politics with business was not a good recipe for success. He carefully avoided taking most political stands in recognition of this principle. By that summer, however, he decided to pursue a new challenge and left his printing business to David Hall.

Franklin was elected to the assembly where he believed he could do much good and that much good was sorely needed. In typical Franklin style, he described his entry to his latest avocation in a forthright way.

> I conceived my becoming a member would enlarge my power of doing good. I would not however insinuate that my ambition was not flattered by all these promotions. It certainly was.

For considering my low beginning they were great things to me. And they were still pleasing as being so many spontaneous testimonies of the public's good opinion, and by me entirely unsolicited.

The public's good opinion was truly merited. If there was an archetype for a Renaissance man, Franklin would be well suited for the title. His pubic-spirited causes numbered many. Added to the Junto, a philosophical society and the Library Company were endeavors involving fire insurance and hospital improvements to go along with his life-improving inventions. When he took his seat in August, he stepped into a world of historical vexations between the Assembly, the proprietary Penn family and, at least for a brief time, his old nemesis Governor Keith, who would be run out of town for his uncured habit of making promises to pay that he did not keep.

Some of Franklin's initial work in the assembly was rather mundane. A few of his committee assignments included considering a tax on dogs and the regulation of the size of a baker's loaf of bread. Eventually the new assemblyman settled on the pursuit of two important initiatives. The more ambitious of the two projects involved expanding the quantity of paper currency, something Franklin had long believed was a necessity to grow the colonial economy.

The other reform was aimed at controlling crime. In this battle for safer Pennsylvania streets, Franklin proposed better street lighting and paid regular constable patrols, complete with duties aimed to target specific types of crime. What could not be ignored, however, was the problem of Great Britain dumping its criminal convicts on the streets of the American colonies.

David Hall editorialized about it in Franklin's old newspaper the *Gazette*. Additionally, Franklin wrote anonymously in his former newspaper, to counter the argument that these wayward souls just needed a new environment and a fresh start that the colonies provided. Franklin likened the rationale to sending Pennsylvania rattlesnakes to London.

> However mischievous those creatures are with us, they may possibly change their natures if they were to change climate. [Then Franklin devised a plan whereby the snakes could be collected for a bounty when they emerged from hibernation.] Then I would prepare to have them carefully distributed in St. James' Park, in the Spring Gardens and other places of pleasure about London; in gardens of all nobility and gentry throughout the nation; but particularly in the gardens of the Prime Minister, the Lords of Trade and Members of Parliament; for to them we are most particularly obliged (for America's felon problem).

The contribution to the crime problem by German immigrants was a much thornier discussion, even by eighteenth-century standards. Franklin viewed the vast amount of these immigrants to be good people and said, "They have their virtues, their industry and frugality is exemplary, they are excellent husbandmen and contribute greatly to the improvement of a country." His real issue with the German immigrants was not so much crime but their laggard assimilation to American culture and participation in its defense. With the ever-present French always a threat, Franklin noted the difficulty of enlisting the German population in support of the provincial militia.

"The Germans, except a very few in proportion to their numbers, refused to engage in it, giving out among one another, and even in print, that if they were quiet the French, should take the country, would not molest them."

Security was never far from the mind of the North American British colonist and beyond the involvement of the French in the equation of power was the important role of Native Americans. Two years into his term in the assembly, Franklin was named to a three-member commission by the Pennsylvania governor along with Richard Peters, secretary of the Provincial Council, and Speaker of the Assembly Isaac Norris. The three were tasked with shoring up relations with the Delawares and other tribes of the Six Nations. The natives were being pinned between the French in the west and the English in the east. Good relations with the tribes was of the utmost importance to the English and Franklin was assigned to the commission as a result of his level-headed common sense.

The Carlisle Treaty, as the talks were called, was more an exchange of desires than a formal agreement with specifics spelled out. The Native Americans complained about English advancement on native lands and the high cost of English goods. The problem of trade was exacerbated by the English purveying flour and rum when the Indians truly desired shot and powder. Franklin witnessed firsthand the destructive nature of the liquor imported by the English, it having the undesirable effect of making its victims "dissolute, enfeebled and indolent," all to the English disadvantage when the tribes would suffer advances by the French. Liquor was forbidden for the Native Americans during the negotiations. Franklin recounted the transaction of business before and after the liquor ban in his autobiography.

> As those people are extremely apt to get drunk and when so are very quarrelsome and disorderly, we strictly forbade the selling any liquor to them; and when they complained of this restriction, we told them that if they would continue sober during the treaty, we would give them plenty of rum when business was over. They promised this, and they kept their promise because they could get no liquor, and the treaty was conducted very orderly and concluded to mutual satisfaction. Then they claimed and received the rum. This was in the afternoon. They were near one hundred men, women, and children, and were lodged in temporary cabins built in the form of a square, just without the town. In the evening, hearing a great noise among them, the commissioners walked out to see what was the matter. We found they had made a great bonfire in the middle of the square. They were all drunk, men and women, quarrelling and fighting. Their dark-coloured bodies, half naked, seen only by the gloomy light of the bonfire, running after and beating one another with firebrands, accompanied by their horrid yellings, formed a scene the most resembling our ideas of hell that could well be imagined.

Franklin's service on the commission that met at Carlisle was only the very beginning of decades of involvement in colonial defense. The next opportunity came soon enough.

> In 1754 war with France being again apprehended, a congress of commissions from the different colonies was by an order of the Lords of Trade to be assembled at Albany, there to confer with the

chiefs of the six nations concerning the means of defending both their country and ours. Governor Hamilton having received this order, acquainted the House with it, requesting they would furnish proper presents for the Indians to be given on this occasion, and naming the Speaker (Mr. Norris) and myself to join Mr. Thomas Penn and Mr. Secretary Peters as commissioners to act for Pennsylvania. The House approved the nomination and provided the goods for the presents, tho' they did not much like treating out of the province, and we met the other commissioners at Albany about the middle of June.

Ever the pragmatic and analytical thinker, Franklin had pondered the difficulties of colonial defense encountered in the last war with France: King George's War fought 1744-1748. He understood that a lack of a coordination of resources and defense amongst the colonies was a significant shortcoming. Franklin saw the need for a plan. Even before the Albany Congress was convened, Franklin devised a scheme and sent it to a number of friends. He also created what is generally credited as the first political cartoon in America and had it published in the *Gazette*. The famous "Join or Die" illustration depicted a snake severed into eight sections, from tail to the head (South Carolina, North Carolina, Virginia, Maryland, Pennsylvania, New Jersey, New York and New England, with each snake section labeled accordingly). Below the cut-up serpent he placed the words "Join or Die," the point being effectively conveyed.

The Albany Congress began on June 19 and adapted a final plan of union on July 10. The final product, subject to the approval of the crown, became known as the Albany Plan. While the plan was never fully adapted, its formulation by a coordinated colonial congress was noteworthy without more. The object in 1754 was not to break with the mother country—quite the opposite—but the mold was cast. A coordinated response to hostility with France was not the only possible application. Just as important was the elevation of Benjamin Franklin to a larger political stage. Franklin emerged from the Congress as a man respected for his ability to skillfully pair well-thought-out solutions to the problems facing the governed. His transition from the business world was complete. Franklin's mission as a budding statesman had many twists and turns ahead; his political life was just beginning.

Chapter 13

Walt Disney Reinvents the American Vacation

Sometime in 1955, Walt Disney will present for the people of the world and children of all ages—a new experience in entertainment."

~ *Walt Disney*

If diplomacy with the Native American tribes and colonial defense, especially with the French in mind, were Franklin's preparation for statecraft on a much bigger stage, then trains, nostalgia and television were Walt Disney's antecedents to revolutionizing the American vacation. While *Cinderella* steadied the studio's finances, it and other content produced at the time did little to challenge Walt's creative urges. Soon a bold concept, something Roy Disney wouldn't initially support, was soon to take shape.

Disneyland doesn't have a precise birthdate. No one knows for sure just when Walt Disney made a clear commitment to build an amusement park. Certainly, there had been a lifetime of influences that contributed to Walt's vision. Some of those experiences were in closer proximity to the planning of Disneyland, and some had long since passed. As early as the Laugh-O-Gram days, Walt visited Kansas City's Electric Park and reportedly told animator Rudy Ising he would build an amusement park someday. At the opposite end of the timeline, Walt visited Denmark's Tivoli Gardens while on location in England for the filming of *The Adventures of Robin Hood and His Merrie Men* during the summer of 1951. In between, there were many Sunday visits with his daughters to worn-down, uninspiring amusement parks that left Walt thinking about a better way.

The cleanliness and quality of the food offerings at Tivoli Gardens impressed Walt enough to borrow $100,000.00 against his life insurance policy to begin planning his own park. He enlisted Harper Goff, an illustrator, to create park renderings and even started purchasing live animals and miniatures in anticipation of his park. As the plan grew and the eleven acres on Riverside became wholly inadequate, money became an acute need. As always, a reluctant Roy had to be won over. Walt's lofty goals required a partner whose firmly planted feet were paired with a mind that knew how to communicate with the stuffed-shirt money folks.

In December 1952, with Roy's guidance, Walt formed a second company, WED Enterprises. Roy helped his brother negotiate a new personal services contract with the studio as well as a new agreement to license his name. With the financial security of a deal with the studio in place, Walt had a new entity ready to accommodate plans for his amusement park, which now had a name—Disneyland.

Even as the concept of an amusement park gathered steam, Walt had begun mobilizing talent. He recruited a staff, including some key people from the studio. Art directors Dick Irvine and Marvin Davis joined Harper Goff, and they were collectively tasked to create some of the original sketches of Disneyland. Walt hired his brother-in-law Bill Cottrell, who worked on both park planning and television projects. His combined scope of work would comprise an important synergy for the park's success. As

13 | Walt Disney Reinvents the American Vacation

early as March 1952, Goff was touring the country, mining ideas for Walt's park. His fact-finding journey included stops at Old Sturbridge Village in Massachusetts, Greenfield Village in Michigan, the Lincoln Museum in Chicago, and Colonial Williamsburg in Virginia.

Walt honed the ideas of his staff, sifting, designing and redesigning, always looking for a way to improve or revise a concept. Once again, Walt was "plussing" ideas just as he did in the early days of animation. Planning for the park revived him. He was thoroughly invigorated by an imagination that was in overdrive. What took shape was a comfortable experience where the rough edges of realty were sanded off and warm nostalgic emotions, common to us all, were polished to a shine. Walt wanted to evoke an emotional response without letting the real world interfere. Walt instructed Goff to draw the scenes from Walt's imagination. Walt talked about a castle, a train station with horse-drawn carriages, and a small-town, turn-of-the-century Main Street complete with shops, a fire station, police station and town square.

Postwar America ushered in a time of change. While possibilities abounded, the country could look back with a strong measure of pride. The American way was a winning way, a credo born in opportunity and success for those who worked hard. Walt's life spanned some of the most important years of the American Republic and he was proud to have lived the American dream. Celebrating it was natural to Walt and a heavy dose of American heritage was a vital element of Walt's amusement park from his earliest thinking about it.

The best-laid plans and greatest innovations could not be executed without money, however. By late summer 1953, Walt's initial capitalization of WED was running low. The idea of financing Disneyland was weighing heavily on his mind. He needed to find a way to maintain the enthusiasm for his amusement park. One can imagine how much he pondered solutions to his money problem that summer.

The answer came suddenly. One night that summer, Walt lay in bed, awake and pensive. The fix was obvious, hiding in plain sight, so to speak. Walt would finance his amusement park with television. In 1953 two-thirds of American households owned a television. The medium that had fascinated Walt since the late 1930s and for which he had already produced special programming, was his path forward. The next day Walt excitedly informed his brother Roy, "Television! That's how we'll finance the park—television!"

Walt Disney was in the process of making entertainment history, the kind that defines a culture, but before he could move forward, he needed board approval. He would need television content to entice a network to help underwrite Disneyland. Walt Disney Productions was a necessary partner, since the studio would provide the content the networks were after. Walt made his pitch to the board of directors, but the board was far from a "rubber stamp" in making the decision. Some of the board members were not convinced that entering two new fields, television and an amusement park, especially at the same time, was prudent. Walt dug in, making a strong case for both endeavors. The way he saw it, television was a powerful outlet to promote the studio's offerings. He had the experience of two television Christmas specials to prove it.

To Walt, the production of Disney films was not enough. The idea of an amusement park may have been

13 | Walt Disney Reinvents the American Vacation

a bold one, but the Disney brand was built on innovation and that's what he intended to do, innovate. Walt made his thoughts plain. "If I'm going to devote that much talent and energy to a television show, I want something to come out of it. I don't want this company to stand still. We have prospered before because we have taken chances and tried new things."

Walt continued his plea, pointing out that Disney was an entertainment company and that didn't limit the company to films. He saw his concept of an amusement park as pure entertainment. As he did when he acted out *Snow White* for his studio staff, he reached down and summoned the depth of his emotions. He described Disneyland this way:

> There is nothing like it in the entire world. I know, because I looked. That's why it can be great because it will be unique. A new concept in entertainment, and I think—I "know"—it can be a success.

Walt ended the summation teary-eyed. Like his brother Roy earlier, the board was enlisted in the cause. Before Roy could go to New York and meet with the networks, however, he needed a tool that did not exist yet.

In the months since WED was organized and during the years before, Walt's Disneyland had gone through many iterations. Through all the planning and modifications, no single schematic design or rendering existed. Disneyland existed largely in Walt's head. Roy would need a design in order to sell network executives who had more in the way of financial resources than creative vision. On Saturday morning, September 23, 1953, Dick

Irvine contacted Herb Ryman, an art director at the Disney studio in the 1940s who had left for a job at Twentieth Century-Fox before going out on his own as an artist. Irvine, long acquainted with Ryman, thought Herb was the right talent for a job with a very short deadline. Irvine told Ryman that Walt wanted to see him at the studio right away. Walt himself got on the phone and asked Ryman how quickly he could get to the studios. Ryman responded fifteen minutes if he came as he was and a half-hour if he got dressed up. Walt opted for the more expedient option.

When Ryman arrived at the studio, Walt had some more convincing to do. Not only did he need a detailed drawing of Disneyland, but he needed it soon, in a matter of hours. The exchange between the men captured for posterity one of the most famous rush jobs in history.

> "Look, Herbie, my brother Roy is going to New York Monday to line up financing for the park. I've got to give him plans of what we're going to do. Those businessmen don't listen to talk, you know; you've got to show them what you're going to do."
>
> "Well, where is the drawing? I'd like to see it."
>
> "You're going to make it."

The deadline was Monday morning and Ryman, shocked over the impossibility of the task, let Walt know it. Desperate, Walt volunteered to stay with Ryman at the studio through the weekend while he worked. Ryman saw no practical value in the offer, but Walt made it with the same teary plea he used with his board of directors—"like a little boy," Ryman later said. He couldn't turn him down.

13 | Walt Disney Reinvents the American Vacation

So, through that September weekend Herb Ryman worked, Walt by his side. An aerial schematic drawing took shape, the artist taking into account prior sketches, drawings and Walt's contemporaneous visions communicated throughout the weekend. Ryman finished his job by Monday morning and Bill Walsh, who Walt had chosen (inexplicably to Walsh) as his first TV producer, wrote a description to go along with the visual.

> The idea of Disneyland is a simple one. It will be a place for people to find happiness and knowledge. It will be a place for parents and children to share pleasant times in one another's company: a place for teachers and pupils to discover greater ways of understanding and education. Here the older generation can recapture the nostalgia of days gone by, and the younger generation can savor the challenge of the future. Here will be the wonders of Nature and Man for all to see and understand.
>
> Disneyland will be something of a fair, an exhibition, a playground, a community center, a museum of living facts, and a showplace of beauty and magic. It will be filled with accomplishments, the joys and hopes of the world we live in. And it will remind us and show us how to make those wonders part of our own lives.

When Roy arrived in New York that September, there were three potential players with whom he could make a TV deal, and in the process, jump-start his brother's dream of a revolutionary amusement park. Somewhat predictably, the two more established networks were cool to Roy's proposal. Far better established than ABC, which had just fourteen primary affiliates, CBS boasted seventy-four affiliates and NBC, seventy-one. CBS President William Paley didn't think that Walt's amusement park would be innovative. It will be "just another Coney Island," Paley quipped. NBC Chairman David Sarnoff, who had won out over CBS to air Disney's 1950 Christmas special, sure wanted the Disney programming, but he didn't have the same yen for the park. "I want your television show, but why the hell do we have to take that damned amusement park?" Sarnoff declared.

That left only one real suitor, the American Broadcasting Corporation (ABC), or what Milton Berle jabbed might better be described as the Almost Broadcasting Company. ABC was headed by Leonard Goldenson, who was relatively new to the television business. Goldenson had gotten his start in the motion picture industry, but he was determined to get into television and bought ABC in 1951. His beginnings were difficult, and the limited number of ABC affiliates made securing advertising harder. ABC needed help and the promise of a Disney television show might just be the panacea, Goldenson judged. Each party needed the other. A deal with Disney for content would provide the ailing network a needed shot in the arm and Disney programming would provide both the studio and the amusement park a good place to promote, all while obtaining the financing to get the park project off the ground.

Roy Disney secured from ABC and Goldenson $500,000 and a guarantee of loans up to $4.5 million for a 35% stake in the park and Disney's promise of a one-hour television series. In early 1954, Walt Disney Incorporated, doing business as WED Enterprises, consisted of four shareholders. ABC owned 34.48%;

13 | Walt Disney Reinvents the American Vacation

Walt Disney Productions owned a like percentage for the same $500,000 investment; Western Printing, a publishing licensee, purchased a 13.79% stake for $200,000; and Walt Disney himself subscribed to 17.25% for a $250,000 investment.

On Wednesday evening, October 27, 1954, Walt Disney's *Disneyland* program premiered on ABC. The opening theme music was "When You Wish Upon a Star" from *Pinocchio*. The show preceded the opening of the amusement park by nearly ten months. In the premiere episode, Walt gave viewers a tour of the Disney studios and then a detailed description of Disneyland, its location, themes and philosophy. He told viewers that *Disneyland* would be a place of hope and dreams, facts and fancy, all in one. Succeeding episodes of Disneyland featured updates on the park given by Walt, complete with descriptions of the different realms of Disneyland including Fantasyland, Adventureland, Tomorrowland and Frontierland.

If anyone doubted the promise of a synergy between Disney, his amusement park and television, that ended with a five-part series that ran in one-hour episodes on ABC from December 5, 1954 through December 14, 1955. *Davy Crockett* was an immediate national sensation. Within days of the series' first episode, "David Crockett, Indian Fighter," the theme song, "The Ballad of Davey Crockett," went to number one on the *Your Hit Parade* radio show and stayed there for thirteen weeks. Seven million records of the ballad were sold in a short six months. Crockett t-shirts and toy rifles joined the licensing product parade, capped off, literally, by the sale of ten million coonskin caps. Walt's programming, produced with a quality ahead of its time, was both a technical and content success with an audience starved for that kind of programming. The merchandising success proved that baby boomers, who comprised the majority of that audience, were starting to drive the family budget.

The frenzy over Davy Crockett could not have been better timed by a man banking on a new form of family entertainment that would lean hard on a sense of national heritage. The nostalgia of small-town America and all the values that might conjure plus just plain family fun was embodied in Walt's programming and plans. America, already embroiled in the Cold War, was more than receptive, not only its own national pride, but to the story of a courageous, backwoods-wise, down-to=earth realist who was out to do the right thing with vigor.

While Disney was changing the television airwaves, another sort of drama had ensued in Anaheim, California. Construction of Disneyland, after years of planning and the recruitment of lots of talent, commenced on December 16, 1954. After almost exactly one year of frantic excavation, building and landscaping, often conducted around the clock, Disneyland opened on July 17, 1955. The novelty of the place was not limited to its physical attributes but also included training methods for staff, known as "cast members," to make the "guest experience" the best it could be. The project exceeded its initial budget by more than three times with an investment of $17 million by the time the gates opened.

There were more than a few hiccups during Disneyland's opening days. Walt had to choose between finishing watercoolers or bathrooms because of a plumbers' strike; he chose the latter. Despite a number of snafus, he wasn't bothered. The live broadcast of the

13 | Walt Disney Reinvents the American Vacation

opening aired on ABC and was hosted by Walt's friend Art Linkletter, along with actors Bob Cummings and Ronald Reagan. It was the most significant live broadcast ever attempted at the time. Ninety million viewers watched a live feed caught by twenty-five cameras. It was uneven at times, but, according to the official Disney fan club, D23, "it went off with relatively few miscues."

The off-camera missteps, traffic jams, counterfeit tickets, inordinate waiting times and a lack of food and drink would be remedied in time. Nonetheless, Walt had a huge success on his hands, of that there was little doubt. He saw a future of constant improvement to the park, something impossible once a film was completed, as an exciting prospect. He now had a place where his audience could not only enter the scene but become a part of it. The fifty-three-year-old Walt Disney had changed America again, adding to the legends of Mickey Mouse and the feature-length animated film. In his opening day speech, he may have reflected upon American's founding fathers. Could they have dreamed what America would become?

> To all who come to this happy place: welcome. Disneyland is your land. Here age relives fond memories of the past, and here youth may savor the challenge and promise of the future. Disneyland is dedicated to the ideals, the dreams, and the hard facts that have created America, with the hope that it will be a source of joy and inspiration to all the world.

Chapter 14

Franklin Takes a Role on a Larger Stage

Much of the strength and efficiency of any government in procuring and securing happiness to the people, depends, on opinion, on the general opinion of the goodness of the government, as well as the wisdom and intensity of its governors.

~ B. Franklin

Benjamin Franklin's life changed in January 1757. The accomplished businessman, inventor, scientist and popular budding statesman was embarking on a new chapter in his life. The mission and its outgrowths would someday put his stamp on the American republic like no one else. Even before the Pennsylvania Assembly appointed him as its agent, he had created a legacy that would be the envy of most. Now that was about to expand by leaps and bounds. Franklin was fifty-one years old when the assembly sent him to London. He was nearly the same age as Walt Disney when Walt incorporated WED Enterprises in furtherance of his dream of an amusement park that would change America. In *The First American: The Life and Times of Benjamin Franklin,* author H. W. Brands wrote, "Franklin's removal to London in 1757 marked a turn in his life no less important than his move from Boston to Philadelphia thirty-three years earlier."

Enlightenment & Enchantment

The French and Indian War, or more precisely, the funding of it, would forever change much about colonial America. Franklin's mission in 1757 was to persuade Thomas and Richard Penn, Pennsylvania's proprietors, of the need for consistent financial support of the colony's troops. By the time of Franklin's appointment by the assembly, the war was already in its third year and the threat to Pennsylvania's security very real. As proprietors, the Penns had a special grip on the colony and its assembly. The exclusive charter granted William Penn by King Charles I was intended to create a strong British hold on the mid-Atlantic seaboard where Swedish and Dutch settlements already existed. It also ensured an agreeable neighbor for the neighboring colony under the control of the Duke of York, the future King James II.

The realities nearly a century later were far different. The Penn family rejected the right of the assembly to tax their land. Their ironic argument held that they had no obligation to pay a levy imposed by the assembly since the proprietors had no vote in the assembly's election. Things were not that simple, however. The colony's governor was controlled by the Penns and reserved the right to abrogate laws passed by the assembly. The majority of the assembly deeply believed in the fairness and equity of the proprietors paying their fair share of the colony's burdens, especially those related to defense.

Franklin's task was a tall order. He came to believe fundamentally that Pennsylvania would be better served if it were a royal colony directly under the control of the monarch. Franklin arrived in Falmouth, England, on July 17, 1775. He would spend the next five years in London attempting to curtail the power of the Penns or at least to obtain assistance from the crown in coercing them to pay a fair share of the taxes levied by the assembly.

14 | Franklin Takes a Role on a Larger Stage

Franklin's meetings with the Penns did not go well. To make matters worse, he suffered from the onset of a debilitating illness. Franklin contracted what he believed was a cold contemporaneously with delivering a list of the assembly's grievances to the Penns. While the cold symptoms subsided, they were replaced with another malady that included a high fever and headaches with a spot on the top of his head that was very hot. A physician bled him from the back of the head, and prescribed a tea brewed from a medicinal bark. The headache pain came in bouts lasting twelve to thirty-six hours and at times sent him into delirium. The illness, which lasted two months, was the second-most serious of his life. His first weeks in London were rather inauspicious.

The Penns did what the wealthy have long done; they resorted to their lawyer, who skillfully and slowly guided Franklin's complaint through a series of government bureaucrats, each siding with the Penns. Eventually the matter found its way to the Board of Trade, advisors to the Privy Council, the final arbiter of the issues between the Penns and the assembly. In June 1760, nearly three years after Franklin first arrived in Great Britain, the Board issued its opinion siding with the Penns. The assembly's grievances then moved to the Privy Council.

The Privy Council hearing occurred at Whitehead in a hearing room called the cockpit, a place where Franklin would experience a far more critical showdown in January 1774. This cockpit hearing, a far milder affair involving the taxation of the proprietors, was conducted in late August 1760. The Privy Council was more conciliatory than the Board of Trade. The council ruled in favor of Franklin on the most important issue, the ability of the assembly to tax the proprietors' estates. All was not lost for the Penns, however. The council exempted much of their land because it was unsurveyed and made sure the taxes levied on them were at the lowest applicable rates.

News of the Privy Council's decree arrived in Philadelphia in January 1761. The assembly did not receive the outcome well and rejected the amendments to their tax legislation which were a part of the Privy Council's order. The funding of the colony's defense would remain a hodgepodge of parliamentary allotments, concessions by the assembly, gratuitous payments by the proprietors, and alcohol taxes. It was no way to run a colony and Franklin was steadfast in his view that Pennsylvania would fare better as a royal colony.

The outcome before the Privy Council effectively concluded the essential tasks of Franklin's agency, but not his stay in London. Ostensibly, he managed the colony's investments in England, though his performance in that regard was lamentable. The real purpose for extending his stay may have been more likely tied to the pleasure of experiencing all of the accolades generated by his celebrity. Philosopher, inventor, writer, and statesman, Franklin had earned great respect beyond the shores of colonial America. He was never one to completely dismiss his own vain impulses. In his autobiography he wrote of vanity, as it was one of his motivations to write it in the first place.

> Most people dislike vanity in others, whatever share they have of it themselves; but I give it fair quarter wherever I meet with it, being persuaded that it is often productive of good to the possessor, and to others that are within his sphere of action; and therefore, in many cases, it would not be altogether absurd if a man were to thank God for his vanity among the other comforts of life.

14 | Franklin Takes a Role on a Larger Stage

Franklin would stay in London for two years subsequent to the Privy Council's decision. During that period, he was awarded a Doctor of Civil Law degree by Oxford University at a convocation held specifically for that purpose. Notably, his social circle included the Scottish philosopher David Hume, Lord Kames, and William Strahan, a Scottish printer, publisher and member of Parliament. All were impressed with the depth and span of Franklin's interests and knowledge. Somehow, he was able to articulate the genius of his thoughts on a matter with language that was simultaneously plain and eloquent.

Franklin's second stay in London, far different than the coming-of-age goose chase Governor Keith had sent him on more than three decades before, molded him into a proud Briton. More than any other American, he had established himself as an international man of enlightenment, something that depended on a deep connection to his British heritage. In fact, he told his friend William Strahan that he would likely make his permanent residence in London sometime soon. As he sailed for Philadelphia in August 1762, nothing would have remotely suggested what lay ahead for Franklin or any notion that someday the American colonies would throw off the yoke of colonial imperialism.

Franklin's stay in Philadelphia would last slightly more than two years. The cost of the defense of the American colonies once again thrust Franklin into a controversy, this time over British Prime Minister George Grenville's plan to raise revenue from the colonies. The British would require the colonies to help defray the cost of their defense in the recently ended French and Indian War. Grenville devised a stamp tax that would be imposed on a long list of paper goods and documents, including licenses, deeds, indentures, leases, newspapers, almanacs, playing cards, dice and the like. Franklin proposed an alternative. In Franklin's plan the levy would be made solely on paper currency, something Parliament had curtailed in the colonies. Franklin reasoned that sort of a tax would mostly impact merchants already used to paying for the cost of money in the form of interest. Grenville's plan would impact all, including many common folks who were not used to paying taxes. The law was wildly unpopular in the colonies from the start and things would progress in the wrong direction.

The law was conceived by Grenville as early as 1763 upon his succeeding the Bute ministry. Parliament formally announced the consideration of a Stamp Act in April 1764. By the autumn of that year, Franklin had lost his seat in the Pennsylvania Assembly. The campaign pitted Franklin against the proprietors and governor. His adversaries were successful in sullying Franklin's reputation by alleging a scheme by him to have himself appointed governor by the crown when Pennsylvania was converted to a royal colony. The election itself is a fascinating look at colonial politics. Franklin was actually running for two seats simultaneously, one in Philadelphia and the other in Philadelphia County. The voting began on October 1 at nine o'clock in the morning. The turnout was heavy and lines long. The proprietors called for the polls to close on October 2 at three o'clock in the morning. Franklin opposed the move and was successful in keeping the polls open for three more hours. It was a fatal mistake. The proprietors descended into Germantown and other neighborhoods and canvassed effectively, rousing several hundred voters of bed. Franklin lost both seats by very narrow margins—in the case of the county seat, the margin was only 19 votes out of 31,000 cast. As it

14 | Franklin Takes a Role on a Larger Stage

turned out, Franklin's loss was likely tied to not only the expansion of the polling hours but also owing to a perceived slight of the German population as a result of a mistranslation of one of his comments.

Franklin thought the whole matter to be so absurd that he suggested, "This is quite a laughing matter." The Penns were not laughing when the Assembly reappointed Franklin as Pennsylvania's agent in London. Franklin set off once again back across the Atlantic on November 7, 1764, ready to lobby against the Stamp Act. His efforts, including his alternative plan to tax only paper currency, were not successful. The Act passed the House of Commons on February 27, 1765, and became law with the assent of the crown on March 22.

In the wake of the passage of the act, Franklin made two missteps. First, he published the body of the Act in the *Gazette,* a newspaper he jointly owned with David Hall until 1766. The Act was published without critical commentary and as a result Philadelphians and folks beyond saw that as a tacit approval of the new law. It was an unpopular move. To complicate matters further, Grenville gave Franklin the right to name Pennsylvania's new stamp commissioner, passing over Thomas Penn for that privilege of being the person charged with the selection. Grenville believed Franklin was the more substantial figure of the two and therefore favored Franklin with the choice. Franklin wasted no time in putting forward his candidate, John Hughes, and Grenville approved the nomination without delay. The selection of Hughes only underscored Franklin's perceived complicity with the Grenville administration.

The reaction in the colonies to the Stamp Act was incendiary. There were protests and legal maneuvers;

Patrick Henry declared the act unconstitutional in the Virginia House of Burgesses. But nowhere did the act cause more clamor than in Massachusetts. In August a mob led by the Sons of Liberty hung the stamp commissioner, Andrew Oliver, in effigy. They then hunted for Oliver, doing much damage to his house in the process. Fortunately for Oliver, he was away but the pressure was effective. He resigned his post the following day. His brother-in-law, Lieutenant Governor Thomas Hutchison, did not make out as well. The mob completely destroyed his home. Hutchinson was lucky to escape without physical harm or worse.

In Philadelphia, Hughes and Deborah Franklin were fortunate to rally friends to their assistance in successful efforts to protect their properties. While Franklin's home did not require repair, the same could not be said about his reputation. The Stamp Act had certainly not courted favor for him through the summer of 1765. In London, Franklin would appeal to reason with British authorities. Franklin knew the riots were counterproductive but believed that a boycott or slackened demand for British goods because of the stamps would have a practical impact and consequences for British merchants. In turn, those merchants would create political problems for Parliament.

George III dismissed Grenville in July 1765 and the Marquis of Rockingham was installed as prime minister to head a coalition government. Rockingham attempted to balance two hard lines, the followers of William Pitt who believed that Parliament could legislate for the colonies but not tax them, and the adherents of Grenville who held fast to the notion that Parliament wielded unlimited authority over the colonies. Franklin entered

14 | Franklin Takes a Role on a Larger Stage

the debate over the Stamp Act by writing several articles for London journals defending the colonial opposition to the act as well as the vast majority of colonists who were moderates seeking redress without mob violence. In turn he began to improve his public image, something of no small consequence to him.

By mid-February Franklin had made an appearance before the House of Commons, where he made an articulate presentation challenging the Stamp Act. He painted an image of colonial obedience and great favor toward the mother country that existed in 1763, and then a decline in those feelings in the wake of the Stamp Act. When asked how Americans viewed Parliament prior to the act, Franklin replied, "As the great bulwark and security of their liberties and privileges." And when a a member of Parliament asked him if that opinion was still held, Franklin stated, "No, it is greatly lessened."

Franklin's testimony was persuasive. His appearance before Parliament was an impressive affair, his testimony given artfully and with great eloquence. It would be a mistake, however, to conclude that Franklin alone was responsible for the repeal of the Stamp Act in March 1766. The British merchant class had a significant role in the process, but nonetheless, Franklin had come a long way from the initial days of the crisis.

Any celebration over the repeal had to be tempered by another measure before Parliament that was passed contemporaneously with the Stamp Act's repeal. The House of Commons voted 275-167 to repeal the Stamp Act but on the same day the body voted unanimously to endorse The Declaratory Act, which confirmed Parliament's plenary authority "to make laws and statues... to bind the colonies and people of America... in all cases whatsoever."

If the Stamp Act brought colonial unrest to a temporary boil, the pot was nevertheless still simmering. In less than a decade, Benjamin Franklin would find himself before the Privy Council with a far different view of his British heritage in a world that was about to change forever.

Chapter 15

Walt Changes the Entertainment World

WHERE: *Disneyland...where there's plenty of room...*

WHEN: *...Wednesday, July 13, 1955, at six o'clock in the afternoon...*

WHY: *...because we've been married Thirty Years...*

HOW: *...by cruising down the Mississippi on the* Mark Twain's *maiden voyage, followed by dinner at Slue-Foot Sue's Golden Horseshoe!*

Hope you can make it – we especially want you and, by the way, no gifts, please – we have everything, including a grandson!

~ Lilly and Walt

Lillian and Walt Disney's thirtieth wedding anniversary was appropriately timed. It is hard to imagine a better way for Walt to celebrate such a milestone. It was both an opportunity to showcase the park of his dreams and gauge his guests' impressions of the place. Walt wore a glow all evening, at one point standing on the restaurant stage alone, silently wearing a broad smile. Apparently, Walt had a few libations to compliment his buoyant mood because many were worried about him driving home. According to Walt's daughter Diane, "They were trying to steal his car keys and everything, but I said, 'Daddy, can I drive you home?' He said, 'Well sure, honey.' No problem at all. He was meek and mild and willing. He just climbed in the back seat of the car. He had a map of Disneyland, and he rolled it up and tooted in my ear as if with a toy trumpet. And before I knew it, all was silent. I looked around and there he was, with his arms folded around the map like a boy with a toy trumpet, sound asleep. I knew he didn't have too much to drink, because the next morning he didn't have a hangover. He bounded out of the house at seven-thirty and headed for Disneyland again."

Four days later the park that had welcomed a handful of family and friends for the Disneys' anniversary party was overrun with celebrity guests and media. The public grand opening, one day later, welcomed no less an onslaught of fun-seekers, the curious and those who wanted to be counted among the first to witness Disneyland. The phenomenon was not a novelty. The attendance topped one million within seven weeks of the opening. The numbers exceeded hopeful expectations by more than fifty percent. As an additional bonus, the customers spent thirty percent more than predicted. To say Walt was riding a wave of success would be an understatement.

The *Disneyland* television series, television's top-rated show, opened its second season on September 14, nearly two months after the Disneyland amusement park debuted. The new season's first offering was *Dumbo*. Walt's successful venture into television wasn't over. On October 3, 1955, Disney had another debut, *The Mickey Mouse Club*. Once again, Disney produced high-quality children's television programing, something the public thirsted for. ABC had a winner on its hands, selling an impressive $15 million in advertising in the show's first season. While the show didn't prove as profitable for

15 | Walt Changes the Entertainment World

Disney, the studio benefited in other ways, including an increase in merchandising sales, especially for the "mouse ears" caps made popular by the new program. The studio also enjoyed receipts from a club magazine and an opportunity to acquaint another generation of children with the company's staple cartoon characters, including Donald Duck, Goofy, Pluto, and of course, Mickey Mouse.

As the sun set on the 1950s, Walt Disney Productions, like the nation itself, had been transformed. America had witnessed unparalleled growth and an unprecedented industrial and commercial expansion, and Disney's advancements were no less impressive. Walt, Roy, and their companies had built an entertainment empire by 1960. The endeavors had produced a wide breadth of studio offerings, including live-action films, cartoon features, shorts, and plays. In addition to all of these were a television series, music publishing, books, magazines, and a broad array of merchandise. To top it all off, there was Disneyland, with a reach that went beyond the borders of the United States and attracted many world leaders as its guests. Famously, Russian Premier Nikita Khrushchev wanted to visit the park but was denied the opportunity when the Los Angeles police chief was wary of security concerns that would be caused by such a visit. Khrushchev had a tantrum like a petulant child and his reaction made international headlines. Many of the world leaders who had the experience of visiting Disneyland saw it as a shorthand study of the American psyche. Their immersion in American culture was as good as any fact-finding trip. If Disneyland exuded an American confidence and can-do attitude, the balance sheet of Walt's companies did nothing to suggest a lack of adherence to that notion.

The revenue of Walt Disney Productions increased $64 million over a decade, from $6 million to $70 million by the time the 1950s ended. The new decade not only portended growing profits but ushered in another entertainment world improvement by Walt Disney. A dispute with ABC led to a lawsuit filed by Disney, challenging the network's ability to bar the studio from offering cancelled shows to other networks, notably the two-season series *Zorro*. In the end, the companies settled the case. The terms were straightforward. Disney bought out ABC's one-third stake in Disneyland for $7.5 million. Walt Disney Productions owned one hundred percent of Disneyland with that purchase. The company's other two original partners, Walt Disney and Western Publishing had sold their stakes earlier.

The split with ABC created an opportunity for Walt. He had long believed that television would eventually incorporate color. Walt was confident enough in his theory to produce his most recent offerings for ABC in color, even though the network broadcast those shows in black-and-white only and the color production was more costly. Once fully freed from ABC, Walt set his sights on NBC as a new broadcast partner. If there was a network to best advance the goal of broadcasting color programming, it was NBC, Walt theorized. Walt's prediction was not without a solid footing. Much of his thinking relied on the fact that industry giant RCA was NBC's parent company.

RCA had been manufacturing color television sets since the debut of its RCA CT-100 model in 1954. The first color TV featured a twelve-inch-wide screen and cost $1,000. That was more than three times the cost of a black-and-white set. It wasn't until 1972 that color television sets would outsell black-and-white ones. Nevertheless, in 1956 NBC aired a number of color

15 | Walt Changes the Entertainment World

episodes of *The Perry Como Show*, becoming the first network to air a live color television show. Walt's vision was as vivid as any color broadcast and once again quite prescient.

On September 24, 1961, Disney's weekly program debuted on NBC with a new title, *Walt Disney's Wonderful World of Color*. The NBC series would last until 1969; during the advent of color television, it became a Sunday-night staple of family viewing. Who could forget Tinker Bell's wand pointed over the show title with the Magic Kingdom's castle in the background as the show's theme music played "The world is a carousel of color..." The show was actually the third iteration of Disney's Sunday evening television programing. The full list includes: *Disneyland*, October 27, 1954–May 14, 1958, ABC; *Walt Disney Presents*, October 3, 1958–June 11, 1961, ABC; *Walt Disney's Wonderful World of Color*, September 24, 1961–March 23, 1969, NBC; *The Wonderful World of Disney*, September 14, 1969–September 2, 1979, NBC; *Disney's Wonderful World*, September 9, 1979–September 13, 1981, NBC; *Walt Disney*, September 26, 1981–September 29, 1983, CBS; *The Disney Sunday Movie*, February 2, 1986–September 11, 1988, ABC; and the *Wonderful World of Disney*, September 9, 1986–present, ABC.

Just as Walt had brought sound to Mickey Mouse and *Steamboat Willie*, he too had the foresight to understand the impact of color on the future of television. It was another in a long line of innovations that underscored an inexhaustible energy to do things differently, something called "plussing," as he referred to it. Disney's domination of television and family motion pictures was preeminent but lacked the kind of Hollywood accolades that other motion pictures in different genres were attracting.

129

Enlightenment & Enchantment

One year before his deal with NBC and his sixtieth birthday, Walt finally landed the rights to a project that had eluded him for two decades. The *Mary Poppins* stories, four in number, were published by English author P. L. Travers between 1934 and 1952. Walt's pursuit of the rights began after reading what were presumably the first three installments with his daughter Diane in 1944: *Mary Poppins* (1934), *Mary Poppins Comes Back* (1935), and *Mary Poppins Opens the Door* (1943). Walt knew instinctively that the stories were quintessential Disney fare. The author thought differently, and Walt and Roy Disney spent years convincing her to license the movie rights to *Mary Poppins*. Even that came with a critical proviso; Mrs. Travers retained the right of script approval for the movie. The movie, coproduced by Robert Stevenson and Don DaGradi, featured an original song by Disney stalwarts and brothers Robert and Richard Sherman. The movie had substantial input from both Walt and Mrs. Travers.

The movie premiered at Hollywood's Grauman's Chinese Theater on August 27, 1964. The audience received it with great enthusiasm and Walt felt confident he had a big hit on his hands. Mrs. Travers was not as confident. Her reaction was as follows:

> After the screening Mrs. Travers approached Walt. "It's quite nice. Miss Andrews is satisfactory as Mary Poppins, but Mr. Van Dyke is all wrong, and I don't really like mixing the little cartoon figures with the live actors. When do we start cutting it?" Walt grinned a terse reply, "The contract says that when the picture is finished, it's my property, we aren't going to change a thing."

15 | Walt Changes the Entertainment World

The movie drew widespread critical acclaim in major newspapers across the country. *The Hollywood Reporter's* review included the following high praise:

> *Mary Poppins* will be one of the year's box office champions, and a hardy perennial as popular and welcome as Santa Claus. The film makes major stars of its two leading players, Julie Andrews and Dick Van Dyke. It makes everyone connected with it bigger and more important. Bill Walsh was the coproducer. Robert Stevenson's direction makes *Mary Poppins* the greatest musical of its kind since *The Wizard of Oz*. The Buena Vista release is an irresistible picture.

Variety chimed in:

> Disney has gone all-out in his dream-world rendition [from the books by P. L. Travers] of a magical English nanny who one day arrives on the East Wind and takes over the household of a very proper London banker. Besides changing the lives of everyone therein, she introduces his two younger children to wonders imagined and possible only in fantasy. Among a spread of outstanding songs [by Richard M. and Robert B. Sherman] perhaps the most unusual is "Chim-Chim-Cher-ee," sung by Dick Van Dyke, which carries a haunting quality. Dancing also plays an important part in unfolding the story and one number, the Chimney-Sweep Ballet, performed on the roofs of London and with Dick Van Dyke starring, is a particular standout. For sheer entertainment, a sequence mingling live-action and animation in which Van Dyke dances with four little penguin-waiters is immense.

The film's quality was well rewarded at the box office, earning worldwide rentals of $44 million in its first run. If all that wasn't enough, Walt finally had the kind of Hollywood recognition at the Oscars he long believed his work deserved. *Mary Poppins* garnered thirteen Academy Award nominations, including Best Picture of 1964. The film won five Oscars: Best Actress (Julie Andrews), Best Original Score (Robert and Richard Sherman), Best Visual Effects (Hamilton Luske, Peter Ellenshaw and Eustace Lycett), Best Film Editing (Colton Warburton), and Best Song ("Chim-Chim-Cher-ee," music and lyrics by Richard and Robert Sherman).

Mary Poppins, like many of Walt's triumphs, had a long course separating his initial conception and the final articulation of his deeply held dreams. The blockbuster film was not the only long-term project that Walt was planning as he approached his sixtieth birthday in 1961. His next dream may have been the most ambitious in a lifetime that could lay claim to some of the greatest advancements in American culture. His vision almost limitless, his passion nearly unquenchable, Walt's energy was unfailing through his final chapter.

Chapter 16

Guiding the Ship of State

We must all hang together, or assuredly we shall all hang separately.

~ B. Franklin

Benjamin Franklin left Philadelphia in 1764 as a proud Briton; he returned on May 5, 1775, as an American. Five days later the delegates to the Second Continental Congress gathered in the Pennsylvania State House. Franklin's condemnation before the Privy Council on January 29, 1774, by Solicitor General Alexander Wedderburn angered the colonial agent, a man of substance and a learned gentleman of the Enlightenment. There was no turning back. Franklin was sixty-nine years old, far from the prime of his physical existence, but like Walt Disney in his later years, still possessed energy and vision that had hardly sagged. Some of Franklin's biggest moments still loomed ahead. His many and varied accomplishments had accumulated in a long list of titles. To that litany he would add one more—revolutionary.

Franklin's voyage home was quite calm, wholly dissimilar to the situation brewing in the colonies. Seventeen days before Franklin's ship was moored in Philadelphia, hostilities and bloodshed had broken out at Lexington and Concord, Massachusetts, between His Majesty's troops and Massachusetts militiamen. The

British losses numbered 270 killed and wounded while American casualties were approximately a third of that number. While Massachusetts was coming to a full boil, Franklin was copiously, and famously, taking water temperature measurements as he plotted with great precision the location of the Gulf Stream.

When Franklin landed in Philadelphia, delegates to the Second Continental Congress were arriving in the city; their formal session was scheduled to open there five days after his arrival. The Congress wasted little time in calling on the colonies' most experienced and senior political mind. The sixty-nine-year-old Franklin became a member of Congress the day after his arrival in Philadelphia. In his first weeks of service, he was sphinxlike, keeping his opinions to himself, and listening quietly. There were members who doubted where Franklin stood or even whether he was paying strict attention to the early proceedings.

Any fact-finding or formative thinking during Franklin's first days in Philadelphia had to include his meetings with George Washington. The most senior and experienced colonial military leader already had a relationship with America's most senior and recognized diplomat that dated back to the French and Indian War. During that war, Franklin pushed for inter-colony cooperation and Washington witnessed firsthand the shortcomings of the British military tactics on the North American continent and the consequences of failing to achieve what Franklin had advocated. They were friends and respected each other's abilities. Now they were called to collaborate on larger issues and on a grander stage.

Washington arrived in Philadelphia just a day before Congress formally convened on May 9, to a military escort complete with bands playing music fit for a supreme commander. Washington and Franklin likely had the first of a series of meetings with each other on the same day at Franklin's Philadelphia home. Washington and Franklin were both reluctant revolutionaries, men with a lot to lose if things didn't work out, men who had long placed a high value on their British heritage.

By early July 1775, Franklin was ready to lead in a demonstrative way, leaving behind forever any public ambiguities as to his position. Though he signed the last-ditch "Olive Branch Petition," he was one of Great Britain's most vocal opponents from that point to the final abyss. A delegates as firm to the cause of independence as John Adams observed of the new Franklin, in a letter to his wife Abigail, "He does not hesitate at our boldest measures, but rather seems to think us too irresolute, and I suppose (British) scribblers will attribute the temper of the proceeding of this congress to him."

Despite the rancor of the remaining months of 1775, most colonists were still not ready for either a full break from the mother country or to indict the king directly for the growing schism. All of that changed with a pamphlet titled *Common Sense,* a wildly popular treatise that assailed the whole concept of monarchy and forcefully and convincingly set Americans on a path of complete separation from Great Britain in January 1776. Franklin's ties to the growing revolutionary spirit in America were extensive. Even the author of *Common Sense,* Thomas Paine, had a strong connection to Franklin since the older man had secured for his younger associate both passage to Philadelphia and a job in a print shop there after the two had met in London.

On June 11, 1776, Congress appointed a committee to draft a possible Declaration of Independence in furtherance of the passage of resolutions introduced by Virginia's Richard Henry Lee four days before. The committee included Thomas Jefferson, Robert Livingston, John Adams, Roger Sherman, and Franklin. The committee selected a Virginian, Jefferson, to be the principal drafter. Franklin, who liked to avoid drafting documents made the subject of public review, became the document's de facto editor. Franklin's most famous edit replaced Jefferson's words, "We hold these truths to be sacred and undeniable" with "We hold these truths to be self-evident." Franklin, ever the figure of the Enlightenment, opted for a word citing reason over religion. The Jefferson draft was in store for a deeper edit than Franklin's between July 2 and July 4, when the final version was approved by Congress. Franklin uttered some iconic words at the momentous event of the document's signing in early August. After appending his large and bold signature, John Hancock observed, "There must be no pulling in different ways. We must hang together." Franklin quickly quipped, "Yes, we must indeed, all hang together, or most assuredly we shall all hang separately."

If Benjamin Franklin had steered the would-be nation abroad and the fledging county at home with the force of his prestige, experience, and reasoned intelligence, he would also be counted on to guide what came next. The European powers had long vied for territory in the New World and the integrity of their colonial possessions. Wars in the New World were extensions of centuries-old conflicts in Europe. No American colonist could have rationally believed their cause of independence would be achieved without the assistance of an ally made possible by a broader European conflict. The Americans would need the French and there was no one better equipped to enlist their assistance than Benjamin Franklin.

On September 26, 1776, Franklin was named to a diplomatic commission charged with securing help from the French to prosecute the war. Thomas Jefferson and Silas Deane rounded out the three-member commission that would seek French financial assistance, arms and supplies as well as a treaty of commerce and alliance. The seventy-year-old Franklin, beset by gout and his advancing years, set sail for France exactly one month later on the USS *Reprisal,* a merchant vessel refitted to serve as one of America's first naval vessels. The hazards of the passage, beyond the normal mishaps attendant to a one-month Atlantic crossing during the eighteenth century, included the British Navy. Franklin, accompanied by two of his grandsons—one who would serve as an unpaid secretary—arrived in France on December 1, 1776. Franklin's mission would prove both difficult and of historic importance.

Franklin made quite an impression on the French people; their government's initial welcome was far more guarded. French thinkers and aristocrats were fascinated by a man who simultaneously represented the "primitive" New World and the high culture of the Enlightenment. He donned a fur cap instead of a powered wig and was as comfortable explaining natural science in accessible terms as giving pragmatic advice of the sort contained in his famous almanac. A man of science, pragmatism and great common sense, he was held in such high esteem by the French as to inspire a host of souvenirs bearing his likeness. The French consumed Franklin-embossed medallions, rings, watches, and snuffboxes, underscoring the immense celebrity of the good doctor.

Franklin's popularity was far more tempered among French government officials who had the sober responsibility of guiding the French ship of state. There is little doubt that the French wished the new American republic success to the detriment of their historic enemy and rival, but the French would not become entangled with an experiment gone badly. As a result, the initial reception of Franklin and the American cause was tepid.

The French Foreign Minister Comte de Vergennes was standoffish, even refusing to grant Franklin and his other commissioners interviews. The French were not wholly uninvolved though. Hoping the Americans would succeed, the French made small, surreptitious loans in an attempt to keep the American army at least modestly equipped and fed. In the end, Franklin needed a military development that would convince the French that an American victory was possible.

That event would come in fall 1777. And if an army relied on soldiers being well equipped, fed, and clothed, something the Americans struggled to do, it may have been a British officer's overindulgence that cost his country a major battlefield failure. By the middle of 1777, the British war strategy involved separating the fractious New Englanders from the remaining colonies. The military operation was straightforward. General John Burgoyne's army would move south from Canada over the Hudson River Valley and meet General Henry Clinton moving north from New York City via the Hudson River. Things did not go as planned for the British.

Burgoyne's lumbering advance was slowed by officers crossing over difficult terrain with supplies that included the luxury of copious amounts of food and drink. At the same time, Clinton was bogged down in New York City and moved north too late to relieve Burgoyne, whose stretched supply lines made his army vulnerable to the Americans. On October 17, Burgoyne surrendered his entire army to General Gates at Saratoga. The British defeat changed everything. Suddenly, Franklin's mission in France got a whole lot easier.

Once the monumental news reached France, Franklin had the leverage he previously lacked. At one point he feigned a possible peace negotiation with a British agent just to make sure the French, and in particular Vergennes, were paying attention. On February 6, 1778, Franklin appeared in Paris to sign two treaties with the French, one recognizing the American state and opening trade between the two countries, the other a military alliance between France and the United States of America. For the occasion, Franklin wore the same coat he had on when he appeared before the Privy Council in January 1775. Cloaked with a bit of subtle revenge, Franklin knew the cause was far from concluded but now the health of the American state was upgraded from critical to guarded condition. He could add to his long list of accomplishments the development of colonial cooperation aimed toward building a new nation free from the shackles of British imperialism. There were battles ahead, military and otherwise, but with the French treaties there was cause for optimism. Franklin had not slowed and like his counterpart in this examination of the lives of two great Americans, energy enough remained for much more to come.

Chapter 17

Taking His Show East

Disney Tells of $100 Million Project
Orlando Sentinel
Tuesday, November 16, 1965

It didn't take Walt Disney long to embark on what would be the last creative journey of his life after Disneyland opened. While Walt wasn't as old as Benjamin Franklin when he began his last major chapter, age was creeping up on him—just how precipitously would not be revealed for another eight years. In 1958, only three years after Disneyland opened, Walt was in deep thought about a second, even grander amusement park. The new park would likely be located in the East, toward the population centers that were feeding some of the demand for Disneyland. Aside from the geographic location of a second park, there were two other considerations that loomed large, lessons fresh from the experience of creating Disneyland.

Disney failed to control the acres of commercial land that ringed his California amusement park. The success of Disneyland spurred a frenzy of development that took advantage of the economic opportunity caused by a constant stream of guests in search of lodging and dining accommodations. Disney watched other entrepreneurs cash in on all the ancillary demand he created with his novel amusement park. Perhaps worse, Walt decried the poor aesthetic impact of unbridled commercialism more dedicated to profits than appearance.

In order to confirm his suspicions regarding the location of a second park, Walt hired a research economist named Buzz Price. Walt would eventually commission four studies related to the location of a second park, one in 1958, two in 1959 and a final examination conducted in 1961. Both of the 1959 reports recommended Florida as the appropriate site for a new park. Two years later, the prior research was sharpened to meet a couple of Walt's primary requirements. The first condition involved available acreage. Walt wanted a spot where he could acquire a large expanse of land, something on the order of 5,000 to 10,000 acres. It was a far cry from the 160 acres that comprised the original plot purchased for Disneyland. Walt wanted to ensure a site that would permit him to control not only the theme park but the environs that would ultimately host the needs of park visitors as well. He would not repeat the California mistake of allowing third parties to control the look of the park's neighborhood or capitalize on his success. Secondly, Walt wanted to stay away from the Florida coast. He didn't want to compete with all of the sun and sand opportunities the state offered. A location away from the coast would keep his park visitors focused on a single-location stay, a brand-new kind of vacation that a Disney park represented.

In 1961, Price divided Florida into five segments and compared the relative advantages of each for a new park location. In the end, an area in central Florida ranging from just south of Orlando and then north toward Ocala seemed to be the prize region for meeting the needs as

17 | Taking His Show East

laid out by Walt. While Florida, and ultimately central Florida, seemed to be the leading location, Walt had not yet ruled out other East Coast locales. He would consider at least three other sites: a parcel on the Canadian side of Niagara Falls, another at the New Jersey Meadowlands, and finally a site in Washington, DC. All were ruled out and all for the same reason—weather. The winter climate and the cold were determined to be nonstarters.

With Florida being the only truly viable East Coast alternative, all that was left for Walt to consider was the potential success of the basic idea—an East Coast Disneyland. If there was anyone bold enough to trust his instincts, it was Walt Disney. His past would suggest he was almost always right about what would appeal to the public. He had an uncanny understanding of people and, like for Ben Franklin, the study of people was a lifelong avocation. The East Coast park, which would ultimately become known as the Florida Project in its beginning and secret stages, was benefited by another East Coast entertainment phenomenon—the New York World's Fair.

In 1960, Walt and his company, WED Enterprises, were approached by Robert Moses to create and build "a children's village" for the World's Fair, four years before its scheduled opening. The prospect of WED's participation in the New York World's Fair of 1964-65 created a fortuitous opportunity for Walt to test the East Coast market—and at someone else's expense, no less. Moses was a powerful figure in New York, a force for urban development who was responsible for a huge part of the city's infrastructure including public highways, public housing, bridges, tunnels, Jones Beach, and the Lincoln Center. Walt was not interested in building a temporary "children's village," but he did see the value in creating pavilions for sponsors participating in the fair.

The theme of the New York World's Fair was "Peace Through Understanding." The fair welcomed visitors during two seasons, April 22 through October 18, 1964, and April 21 through October 17, 1965. Fairgoers could visit 140 pavilions sponsored by thirty-six foreign countries, twenty-one states and a long list of US corporations. Walt saw advantages in WED's involvement in designing and building fair attractions beyond testing the East Coast market. Corporate exhibits would provide WED valuable opportunities to research and develop new technologies with the help of corporate investments. Moreover, the innovations would provide valuable public relations for Disneyland as well as the actual attractions when they were broken down and shipped west once the fair concluded. Walt entered into talks with a number of American companies. The first of those to commit to WED for an exhibit was Ford Motor Company.

Walt's first entreaty to Ford involved one of his favorite ideas—a Hall of Presidents. Walt envisioned a representation of America's highest office using audio-animatronic figures reenacting the presidents, some of whom would speak for themselves. Disney's use of audio-animatronics employed a complex series of prerecorded sounds and movements to bring an inanimate object to life. The idea of replacing humans or animals with lifelike functioning figures was something that long fascinated Walt. He had experimented with the concept since the early 1950s but its first appearance in a Disney attraction occurred at Disneyland's Enchanted Tiki Room in 1963. To this day, the Enchanted Tiki Room is a feature at Disneyland and at Disney World as well. The display of audio-animatronic birds, led by four lifelike macaws—José with a Mexican accent; Michael, who has an Irish

17 | Taking His Show East

brogue; Pierre, speaking with a French accent; and the Germanic Fritz—has entertained countless parkgoers for decades. Walt sought to improve and create a further use of the technology with a Hall of Presidents for the Ford exhibit.

Ford didn't buy Walt's pitch for a Hall of Presidents, but they became the first company to commit to a deal with Disney for its pavilion. The attraction featured one hundred and sixty 1964 Ford convertibles transporting guests on a twelve-minute automated ride through history. The car radio, capable of broadcasting in four languages, provided narration to go along with a trip through recorded history. While Walt didn't get his Hall of Presidents from Ford, the journey through man's growth and development employed a cadre of audio-animatronic figures.

Another Disney-created pavilion, this time for General Electric (GE), had as its design genesis Thornton Wilder's *Our Town*. John Hench, an imagineer (a Disney term for someone employed for creative engineering), saw a Broadway performance of Wilder's play, in which the narrator talks his audience through multiple generations of life in a small town. WED's final design included a sitting area, designed like a carousel, rotating around and past four fixed stages, each a nostalgic depiction of American life. Each stop along the way featured a look at technological advances, principally through home appliances. The stages were designed to depict the dawn of the twentieth century, the 1920s, the 1940s and finally the twenty-first century (in the most recent iteration of the attraction). The story on each of the four stages was delivered by audio-animatronic figures.

Walt, always a proponent of nostalgia, had a big part in the creation of the GE exhibit. The carousel and its iconic theme song written by Disney's Sherman brothers, the most recent of which begins, "There's a great big beautiful tomorrow shining at the end of every day" evokes a positive spin on society's evolution. The Carousel of Progress is the longest-running stage show in the history of American theatre and continues to entertain guests at Walt Disney World in Florida to this very day. Joe Fowler, valued construction consultant to Disneyland and Disney World, once said, "There was more of Walt in the Carousel of Progress than in anything else we've done." That is just perhaps a good deal of the reason that six decades later, the carousel still turns with every bit of nostalgia Walt intended and has come to represent a part of Walt himself.

As the fair grew closer, two "Disney-inspired" pavilions left Walt unfulfilled. He continued to search for a sponsor for the Hall of Presidents, even entering into discussions with the Under Secretary of State who was in charge of the United States Pavilion, as well as with a number of corporations. Walt's fascination for bringing robots to life was deep. In addition to that interest, Walt had a deep admiration of Abraham Lincoln. As a result, he continued to develop a full-sized Lincoln robot, sponsor or no sponsor, for his Hall of Presidents.

The results of his team's work on the audio-animatronic Lincoln were nothing short of stunning. Certain outsiders were treated to a look at the Lincoln robot, including Robert Moses and Fairfax Cone, the chairman of the commission planning the Illinois exhibit already themed as "The Land of Lincoln." Cone was overwhelmed by the experience of "meeting" Disney's Lincoln. Walt needed to negotiate his fee with the commission, which took a few rounds of discussion, as

17 | Taking His Show East

well as convince some of the members that the final feature would not be "macabre" or underwhelming. Walt's reputation was on the line. The final product performed for parkgoers five times per hour, bringing to bear its 250,000 combinations of movement along with audio inspired by some of the sixteenth president's most important speeches. Some of the audience confused the audio-animatronic Lincoln for a live actor. It was abundantly clear that WED imagineers had delivered on Walt's promise.

The fourth and final pavilion created by Disney for the World's Fair began even before Walt had completed his arrangements with the Illinois Commission. The last of the Disney-created pavilions came in the waning days of preparations, nearly too late to be seriously considered. Pepsi-Cola planned a collaboration with the United Nations International Children's Fund (UNICEF) but made little progress toward any concrete plans. By the time Pepsi contacted Disney, there was just a bit more than a year remaining before the fair's opening day. The challenge was exacerbated by a modest budget, and Joe Fowler told the Pepsi people it just wasn't possible. Walt intervened, making it emphatically understood that it was his decision, and the project was a go.

Fresh from the sober commitment, Walt gathered his designers and described his vision of "a little boat ride we can do." The reaction of the assembled might suggest more accurately that they thought they were the ones on a boat ride. For his part, Walt was enjoying the extra dose of adventure from attempting the nearly impossible challenge. He had no doubt his company would yet again prevail when the task was almost impossible. The boat ride would take visitors through a canal bounded on both sides with the familiar landscapes of the world, from the Eiffel Tower to the gondolas of Venice. The highlight, however, was the children of the world, outfitted in their national dress, all singing in harmony a Sherman brothers song written for the exhibit, "It's a Small World." If that tune is lingering with you right now, it's an experience common to many of the 135,000 daily visitors during the fair and countless more folks in the ensuing six decades since the fair ended and the ride lived on at Disneyland and Disney World.

Even before the fair opened in April 1964, Walt's tangible preparations for a Florida park were underway, including a trip on November 17, 1963, by private jet with a group of Disney executives to scout land parcels. The group left Florida on the fateful day of November 22, 1963. When the jet took off Walt directed the pilot to circle an area south of Ocala. From the window, Walt looked down and spied the highways conveniently accessing an expanse that Walt confidently chose. "That's it!" he said. The plane made a stop in New Orleans to refuel on the return trip to California. It was there the travelers learned of President Kennedy's assassination. It was a quiet trip home, but the purpose of the trip was fulfilled. Walt knew he had his location just a few months before his fair exhibits would be revealed to the public.

Walt was in New York on April 20, 1964, just two days before a throng of guests came to the Flushing Meadows neighborhood of Queens, New York to take in the long-awaited World's Fair. Walt strolled the still-quiet fairgrounds with his company's legal counsel Robert Foster. While Foster was treated to some sneak peeks, his primary purpose that day was not to take in the fair. Foster and Walt were assembling a legal team that would

17 | Taking His Show East

be tasked with secretly buying a large tract of land in Central Florida. Foster was in New York to meet Ralston "Shorty" Irvine, a partner in the New York law firm of Donovan, Leisure, Newton and Irvine. If secrecy was one of the team's objectives, Walt's selection of the firm could not have been made without notice of the law firm's William Donovan's prior service. Donovan was one of the CIA's founders during the World War II era. Part of Irvine's job was to vet and hire a Florida attorney. Irvine selected Paul Helliwell, an old colleague of Donovan's in the CIA. The Florida Project would be guided by people who knew something about keeping secrets. And if the Florida Project was top secret, Walt's successes in 1964 were certainly not.

Results from the fair as well as the 1964 Disney movie *Mary Poppins* did nothing to dissuade Walt, or anyone else at Disney, to cool the Florida project in any way. Total attendance at the New York World's Fair numbered 51.6 million people. The vast majority of those folks, 47 million, took in a Disney-created exhibit, a stunning success by any measure. Taking those highly successful exhibits back to California for inclusion at Disneyland was no small benefit to Disney either. The *Mary Poppins* film, which was the highest-grossing Disney film at the time, together with Disneyland-generated revenue, put the company on a solid financial course for the future.

If 1964 was a pinnacle of sorts for Walt Disney, it was also a time to take stock. Whether Walt had any specific sense of the time he had left could only be speculation, but he was less than three years away from his death. Whatever he sensed, legacy was very much on his mind. He wanted there to be a continuation of his vision—a path forward for a way of thinking that involved both imagination and a constant need to improve. At one point he confessed to story man and sketch artist Bill Pete some of his inner thoughts. "You know, Bill, I want this Disney thing to go on long after I'm gone." Walt hoped his ideas and all he built would be transcendent. He had changed the American entertainment landscape and the culture with it. All that remained was the test of time.

As with Franklin, even the last chapters of his Disney's life were filled with a sense of contribution. There was never a minute wasted. There would be no cessation of constructive activity; only death would halt the yearning to achieve. It is true of both Franklin and Disney that some of their greatest challenges were in fact their last. Each man used all his time to his best advantage, writing with it his story until the last drop of life's ink left his pen.

Chapter 18

Making Peace

There was never a good war or a bad peace.

~ B. Franklin

Bloodshed at Lexington and Concord and at Bunker Hill commenced an eight-year conflict that pitted British regulars against an army they could neither contain nor defeat. Washington was unable to deal the British any sort of decisive blow until French naval assistance helped bottle up Lord Cornwallis at Yorktown. Exhausted and frustrated by what became an expanded war with the French, the British finally entered into a treaty in 1783 recognizing the free and independent States of America. The treaty was negotiated by Franklin and his two other peace commissioners, John Adams and John Jay.

Nothing in the peace negotiations would go on without the notice or approval of Franklin. Franklin's love and aptitude for the game of chess was no secret in the later years of the eighteenth century. One the eve of negotiations between Franklin, his fellow commissioners and their British counterparts, Franklin published his reflections on chess. The essay "The Morals of Chess" was produced by Franklin's Passy press, a small printing press he maintained in his living quarters on the property of Monsieur de Chaumont in Passy, a village on the outskirts of Paris. Franklin wrote:

> Life is a kind of chess in which we have often points to gain, and competitors and adversaries to contend with, and in which there is a vast variety of good and evil events that are, in some degree, the effects of prudence or the want of it.

Quite pointedly, Franklin, sensing his audience might include the British negotiators noted:

> If you have incautiously put yourself into a bad and dangerous position, you cannot obtain your enemy's leave to withdraw your troops and place them more securely; but you must abide all the consequences of your rashness.

The negotiations began in April 1782, six months after the British defeat at Yorktown. The multiplicity of parties, including the French and Spanish, made matters far more complex. The treaty of alliance between the United States and France did not permit for a separate peace for the new American republic, but that did not dissuade the British from attempting to do just that. Complicating matters further, many, including his fellow commissioners, saw Franklin as far too cozy with the French. Franklin was naturally distrustful and if that included both the British and French, he distinguished between the two based on the latter nation's contributions to the American republic.

Franklin had good reason to doubt British intentions. British espionage targeted the good doctor and employed Edward Bancroft, a native of Westfield, Massachusetts,

18 | Making Peace

to conduct it. Bancroft had befriended Franklin while he was a young man in London. Franklin helped Bancroft get his start there, recommending him for a job as reporter on American politics to a British periodical. Bancroft operated as a double agent, feeding the British with intelligence on America's war efforts and communications with European powers, all as a resident of the same house as Franklin. The British valued Bancroft's information during the peace process as well and even raised his compensation.

The British understood that the American they needed to convince was Franklin. During the earliest entreaties by the British, Franklin's fellow commissioners weren't even present; John Adams was in Holland and John Jay was in Madrid. Neither Adams nor Jay had much success drawing the Dutch or Spanish into an American alliance during the war and were still in those nations during the first months of peace negotiations.

Without the French, Franklin exercised caution on how deep into discussions with the British he would proceed. From afar, his fellow commissioners did not necessarily share Franklin's reluctance. Adams and Jay were skeptical of the French, believing the country was concerned about its own interests solely and that any affection for the American republic was a mere illusion. The British negotiators were Richard Oswald and Thomas Greenville, the son of George Greenville—the prime minister who Franklin quarreled with over colonial policy and in particular the Stamp Act.

Though Franklin made it clear any agreements could not be made until his fellow commissioners were consulted, there was one dictate on which Franklin was resolute, American independence. Franklin wholly rejected any notion that the thirteen states would enjoy some form of autonomy within the British empire. As far as Franklin was concerned, the reality of American independence was a fait accompli, something achieved on the battlefield. It was not even a question. The other feature of the earliest talks concerned Canada.

Great Brittan had waged a six-year war against its former American subjects. Franklin made clear that the war was unjust and had cost Americans dearly. Homes were burned, whole villages destroyed, and crops ruined—for this there had to be recompense. Franklin thought fair reparations might lead to the establishment of future commerce and trade between the two nations. When pressed by his British counterparts as to what fair reparations might entail, Franklin answered, "Canada." It was a bold statement to which the British negotiators had little initial reaction. There was virtually no chance that the British would cede Canada to the Americans as part of a peace pact.

The question of a separate agreement between the Americans and the British was very much on the minds of the latter contingent. At one juncture, Greenville acknowledged Franklin's edict relative to American independence. Greenville agreed that America had in fact achieved its goal of independence and therefore there was no reason to continue fighting. America, according to Greenville, must separate itself from France or risk getting drawn into a larger conflict that would not serve American interests.

As summer turned to fall, Vergennes' appetite for war was waning. The machinations of European powers and the reality of various alliances or the lack thereof were not contributing to any advantages for France in continuing the war. As a result, Vergennes encouraged the Americans to seek their own treaty with the British, as would the other European powers involved in the war. The war had taken its toll on the British treasury and once British intelligence was aware of France's new position, there was great incentive for the British to negotiate in earnest.

Franklin and his fellow commissioners began formal discussions with the British on September 27, 1782. Two months of negotiating ensued. Both Adams and Jay were not only concerned about the British commissioners but their own fellow commissioner as well. Adams, especially, viewed Franklin as being cunning and looked at him with a measure of distrust. Nonetheless, Franklin set the essential terms of a peace framework and any fight with his fellow commissioners over the nature of the negotiations failed to materialize. Franklin was happy to leave the hairsplitting to Adams and Jay. The back-and-forth lasted a month and by the end of November, the parties reached an agreement that both sides could support. The terms included all of the conditions that were fundamental to Franklin.

Preliminary articles were signed between the British and Americans on November 30, 1782. Those articles included:

- Formal recognition of a new and independent nation, the United States of America.
- Defined the United States border, including granting the Northeast territory to the United States.
- Secured fishing rights for the Americans to the Grand Banks and other British-Canadian waters.

- Opened the Mississippi River to navigation by the Americans and British.
- Confirmed debts between American and British creditors.
- The United States would help restore the property of loyalists lost during the war.

The treaty was preliminary since it would not be effective until the French signed a similar treaty with the British. France reached their preliminary articles with the British on January 20, 1783. The formal peace treaty was signed in Paris on September 3, 1783.

What Franklin accomplished was, in his view, not limited to the creation of a new nation. For Franklin, the underpinnings of the revolution were much larger than self-rule. He saw the American Revolution as a fundamental expression of the rights of man. Franklin was at the forefront of those who extolled liberty as a virtue that was transcendent. Franklin's primary object of study, not unlike Walt Disney, albeit for different reasons, was undoubtedly people. Franklin wanted to believe in people and their capacity for virtue. He saw the American cause as far-reaching. "Our cause is the cause of all mankind... we are fighting for their liberty in defending our own," he once said. The American Revolution embodied the concept of freedom. Liberty could not be had without a foundation of freedom, and Franklin once said, "Only a virtuous people are capable of freedom. As nations become more corrupt and vicious, they have more need of masters."

The American Revolution would soon reverberate elsewhere. Some of those very masters would be overthrown. All that was left for Benjamin Franklin was to ensure the new nation would in fact embody the idea of liberty. He needed to affirm that primary goal. He had raised liberty from its fledgling birth and helped sustain it as one of America's greatest founders. Now he would set a course for the future, creating a framework of American government that would pay homage to the phrase he had refined more than a decade before: "We hold these truths to be self-evident..."

Chapter 19

Walt's Last Dream

But the most exciting and by far the most important part of our Florida Project...in fact, the heart of everything we'll be doing in Disney World...will be our Experimental Prototype Community of Tomorrow! We call it EPCOT.

It's like the city of tomorrow ought to be. A city that caters to the people as a service function. It will be a planned, controlled community, a showcase for American industry and research, schools, cultural and Educational opportunities.

~ *Walt Disney*

If Benjamin Franklin's last task, the fulfillment of the promise of an American Republic waited, Walt Disney would not see the realization of his Florida project. Death came quickly. In October 1965, Walt appeared in a promotional film pitching the concept of his primary hope for the Florida project, EPCOT, an acronym for Experimental Prototype Community of Tomorrow. The filming taxed Walt physically. It became apparent that the sixty-four-year-old Walt Disney was in some kind of decline.

During the filming of the EPCOT piece, Walt became winded and required the administration of supplemental oxygen between takes. He was tired and looked it. Added to the general fatigue was pain. He was suffering the aftereffects of an old polo injury and his neck and leg were causing him trouble. Not one who was fond of doctors, Walt was finally convinced to consult a specialist to seek relief for his neck pain. Surgery to correct a nerve impingement, thought to be routine, was scheduled for November 11 at the UCLA Medical Center in Los Angeles.

The neck surgery never happened. Preoperative testing revealed a walnut-sized mass on Walt's left lung. The public was not updated about the ominous finding and was told that Walt was in the hospital for tests related to his old polo injury. Walt was immediately admitted to Saint Joseph's Hospital, across the street from his studio, to follow up on the dire X-ray report. Surgery confirmed Walt's worst fear: he had a malignant tumor that had metastasized. Nearly a half-century of cigarette smoking, something that started during his ambulance corps days in France, had caught up with him. Doctors suspected he had no more than six months to live.

Walt was discharged from the hospital on November 21 and made a studio visit to catch up on the status of a number of projects. The studio staff greeted him enthusiastically, though their smiles could not conceal an inner concern about their frail, weathered chief. Sensing their worry, Walt tried to set a tone allaying concerns and, consistent with the warm welcome they gave him, joked, "You'd think I was going to die or something." Walt met with a number of employees that day and each parting had an unspoken question—would it be a last meeting? Before being driven home to rest, he told Hazel George, "There is something I want to tell you." The words never came but the two embraced, no words were necessary between them. She was Walt's closest confidant.

19 | Walt's Last Dream

The official public statement on Walt's post-surgery condition suggested a portion of his lung was removed as a result of a lesion that had caused an abscess. The darkest details were omitted. If there was anything uppermost on his creative mind at that time it was EPCOT. Walt told his son-in-law Ron Miller that if he could live fifteen more years, EPCOT would surpass anything he had done in his career. At the time, the realization of EPCOT, not quite the way Walt envisioned it, was seventeen years in the future. That didn't stop Walt from mentally sketching the visionary community on the ceiling tiles of his hospital room as he patiently explained his concepts to his brother Roy, after he had returned to the hospital the day after Thanksgiving, on November 25. Pain had prompted Wal's hospital readmission. The brothers talked for hours that night. It was the last night of Walt Disney's life. Walt, who celebrated his sixty-fifth birthday in the hospital on December 5, died on December 15 at 9:35 a.m.

Walt was already gone by the time his wife Lillian, their daughters, and sons-in-law arrived at the hospital that day. Walt's daughter Diane remembered that when she arrived her Uncle Roy was massaging one of her father's feet, softly talking to him as if Walt could hear his every word, "Well, kid, this is the end I guess." One of Walt's nurses wrote to the family that in his final days, "the poor man was so fearful." It is not hard to imagine a man like Walt Disney having difficulty embracing his own death. His life was filled with purpose. Absent was any sense of resignation, though he had already accomplished enough to fill ten lifetimes. If changing the entertainment industry and with it a swath of American culture didn't satiate the sixty-five-year-old man, there is little to suggest he was ready to part from the mortal world. And if Walt had gotten those fifteen extra years, it is hard to imagine just what magic would have ensued. That's a question no one can answer.

Those he left behind, both family and staff, were devastated. The staff was an extension of family to Walt, as they together were on a mission to create happiness. The world was in shock, wholly unprepared for the man who created legends to become one himself. The country and world mourned Walt Disney. There is little doubt that he changed not only America but the world. The accolades in newspaper editorials and remembrances had little precedent. The *Los Angeles Times,* in a lengthy obituary, noted:

> A French magazine once proposed Disney for the 1964 Nobel Peace Prize. His chronicles knew no policy, and received affection from the young at heart of whatever political persuasion or ideology.

Admiral Joseph Fowler, vice president of Disneyland, prepared a letter of remembrance for Disney employees. It was not widely circulated but appeared in a company newsletter called "Inside Disneyland." The Disney History Institute released it in December 2014. It read in part:

> Walt Disney's passing is a personal loss not only to each of us, but to people all around the world. Walt's entertainment brought a smile and a laugh into their daily lives. He made their dreams come true.
>
> To all of us at Disneyland, Walt was even more than the "Showman of the World." To us, he was a catalyst, a driving force, and always just plain "Walt." His death leaves an emptiness that can never be replaced.

19 | Walt's Last Dream

The New York Times editorial noted Walt's contribution to wholesome American fun: "That is what Walt Disney gave to us and the world, and it is all summed up in that engaging mouse named Mickey." The simple joy of Walt's years on the family's Missouri farm shaped him. Those emotions ran deep. Sharing them, shaping them and yes, recreating them with all the depth of his imagination was his life's work. In 1960, Walt had returned to Marceline for the dedication of an elementary school in his name. During his speech he said:

> I'm not modest, I'm scared. I'm not funny. I hide behind the mouse, the duck and a lot of other things. I'm still a farm boy – a small-town boy.

Before his death, that small-town boy had kicked off the most significant entertainment venue the world would ever see. With the land acquisition accomplished, Walt Disney officially confirmed a few weeks of speculation in the *Orlando Sentinel Star* newspaper at a press conference held with Florida Governor Haydon Burns at the Equestrian Room of the Cherry Plaza Hotel in Orlando on November 15, 1965. Seven hundred people packed the press conference. Walt briefed the crowd on what he wanted to accomplish:

> Well, Mr. Governor, this has been a wonderful reception that you've given us here. All the faces seem friendly and feel very much at home. This is a big exciting project for us too, you know. In fact, it's the biggest thing we've ever tackled and I'd like for the benefit of the press. I would like to explain that my brother and I have been together for 42 years now.

He's my big brother and he's the one when I was a little fellow went with some of my wild ideas and he was the one to straighten me out, put me on the right path or something or if he didn't agree with me. I'd work on it for years until I got him to agree with me. But I must say that we've had our problems that way but that's been the proper balance that was needed in our organization. He watches out for the financial side of it, the corporate side.

On this project though I'd just like to say I didn't have to work very hard with him on this project. He was with me from the start. Now, whether that's good or bad I don't know. But I think that having the enthusiasm on the part of our whole organization and on the part of the people of the state of Florida really is a good start.

We hope what we develop here will be a real credit to the state, credit to the Disney organization and I might say that when we were planning Disneyland, we hoped that we could build something that would command the respect of the community. And, after 10 years, I feel we have accomplished that not only for the community, but the country as a whole.

And that is actually what we hope to do here is to really develop something...more than an entertainment enterprise. It's something that contributes in many ways. Well, educationally. One thing that is to me the important thing is the family and if you can keep the family together with things. That has been the backbone of our whole business. Catering to the families. That's what we hope to do.

19 | Walt's Last Dream

After Walt's death, Roy Disney took up the mantle that was Disney World. Like so many times in the four decades they were in business together, Roy had a steady hand on the tiller, quickening the process that would culminate in the realization of another one of his younger brother's dreams. The official construction of Disney World's Magic Kingdom got underway in May 1967. Eighteen months and four hundred million dollars later, the park was completed. Nine thousand construction workers labored to turn swampland into the Seven Seas Lagoon and build a theme park steeped in fantasy, nostalgia, and the dreams of tomorrow.

The Magic Kingdom first welcomed guests on October 1, 1971. The park's very first guest was led down Main Street in a grand parade by Mickey Mouse himself. The park was formally dedicated on October 25. Standing next to Mickey Mouse, Roy read his dedication speech, giving full measure to the realization of his brother's dream.

> Walt Disney World is a tribute to the philosophy and life of Walter Elias Disney...and to the talents, the dedication and the loyalty of the entire Disney organization that made Walt Disney's dream come true. May Walt Disney bring joy and inspiration and new knowledge to all who come to this happy place...a Magic Kingdom where the young at heart of all ages can laugh and play and learn—together.

The spot from which Roy delivered his dedication is today commemorated by a bronze statue of Roy seated on a park bench holding Minnie Mouse's hand, thought to be a metaphor for the quiet, steady support he provided his brother and partner. Less than two months after the dedication of Walt Disney World, Roy was dead. He passed away on December 20, 1971, surviving his younger brother by five years and five days. He died at Saint Joseph's Hospital in Burbank, California, the same hospital where Walt passed away.

It is said that while touring the Walt Disney World construction site in an open jeep, Roy would sometimes look skyward and exclaim, "Walt, what have you gotten me into?"

Chapter 20

Building a Nation

Our New Constitution is now established, everything seems to promise it will be durable; but, in this world, nothing is certain except death and taxes.

~ B. Franklin

Benjamin Franklin had done his part in winning the war and negotiating the peace. Nevertheless, much work remained to be done. Building a new nation would prove just as difficult as throwing off the yoke of the British. America's first try at a national system of government proved unworkable. The Articles of Confederation failed to consolidate any real federal authority. The lack of a strong central government and a postwar economy in shambles threatened to unravel the American republic before it even got a real start.

The greatest rumblings came in Massachusetts and in particular the counties of Worcester and Hampshire. In the years 1784 and 1785, over 4,000 legal claims were brought in the Worcester County Court for the collection of debts at a time when the total population of the county numbered less than fifty thousand. Many farmers suffered under a crushing burden of taxes, private debt, court costs and legal fees.

The economic crisis was heightened by the refusal of creditors to accept paper money or barter for the payment of debt. Farmers were forced to pay their debts with silver or gold specie. Under these difficult constraints, farms and property were being seized at an alarming rate. Further compounding the problem, many of the indebted farmers were veterans who had not been paid for their services by their state or the congress under the Articles of Confederation. By August 1786, more than fifty towns sent leaders to a meeting at Hatfield, Massachusetts. Grievances were aired and reforms proposed, but nothing was achieved to ameliorate the growing crisis.

In late August an organized force prevented the Hampshire County Court from sitting at Northampton. Days later, on September 5, another group prevented the Worcester County Courts from opening as well. Other protests in Massachusetts successfully closed courts in Great Barrington, Concord, and Taunton. American patriot James Warren wrote John Adams on October 22, expressing this sentiment: "We are now in a state of anarchy and confusion bordering on Civil War." None other than Sam Adams, incendiary leader of the American Revolution, helped draft a riot act to put down the protesters, drawing a distinction between rebellion in a republic, versus against a despotic monarchy. Adams argued the leaders should be put down with executions.

The federal government lacked the capacity to respond to the Massachusetts rebellion. The insurrection was named for Daniel Shays, a rebel leader who was a veteran of the American Revolution. Governor Bowdoin raised private funds from more than one hundred merchants to fund a militia of three thousand. The militia was put under the command of former Continental Army General Benjamin Lincoln. Most of those who answered the call for service were from the state's eastern counties.

Shays' Rebellion came to a head on January 25, 1787, when the rebel forces attacked the Federal Armory at Springfield. The armory was defended by the militia's General William Shepherd, who ordered grapeshot be fired at the insurgents from two cannons. The volley killed either three or four (this point is debated) rebels. The rebel advance was stopped, and they fled north to Amherst. General Lincoln led his forces west from Worcester and chased the rebels to Pelham and Petersham. Many were eventually dispersed to Vermont and New Hampshire. An advance guard encountered an encampment of insurgents at Petersham. On a bitterly cold night the rebels were surprised in their beds. They surrendered without a shot being fired.

The lasting impact of Shays' Rebellion was the inescapable conclusion that a weak central government, a consequence of the Articles of Confederation, could no longer serve the national interest. The rebellion convinced many of the country's leaders, most notably George Washington, to lend their credibility to an extra judicial convention, a constitutional convention aimed at creating a new, more powerful central government to serve the country.

Washington would have a partner in the pursuit of a more effective government for the new nation. Benjamin Franklin was just as indispensable to righting the ship of the American Republic as Washington. They were easily the two most respected delegates to attend the Constitutional Convention in Philadelphia in May 1787. Even before the convention convened, Thomas Jefferson once said that Washington and Franklin were "on one side (of the Revolutionary cause), and the residue of mankind on the other."

Franklin was the elder statesman, the sage who was at the heart of decisions made at all critical crossroads faced by Americans even before Americans viewed themselves as separate from the British empire. The respect he earned from his contemporaries, most of whom were younger, cannot be underestimated. Once again Franklin was called upon to draw on his experience and prestige in collaboration with a man whose talents had long complemented his own. Franklin was not panicked by the events of Shays' Rebellion, but he saw a growing impetus for change. The gathering momentum was an opportunity. He was keenly aware that efforts needed to proceed with great care.

In anticipation of what was to come in Philadelphia that spring, Franklin organized a group called "The Society for Political Inquiries." That eighteenth-century think tank met in the library of Franklin's new home. On of the group's key members wasn't in Philadelphia at all, but Franklin knew his prestige was indispensable for the process. Washington was made an honorary affiliate, and though hesitant to take a leadership role in the coming convention, Franklin knew Washington's leadership could not be overlooked. Franklin wrote the general, telling him, "Your pressure will be of the greatest importance to the success of the measure." If there was anyone who could convince Washington to throw his weight behind the cause, it was Franklin. And that's exactly what Franklin did.

Washington arrived in Philadelphia to a warm greeting that included an escort into the city by a group of veteran officers who rode out to meet him. Citizens assembled, church bells rang out, and Philadelphia's leaders sought to pay homage to the beloved Washington. There was one stop Washington had to make once inside the city. Washington called on Franklin. The country needed their leadership once again and both men knew it. They also understood that they needed each other. Working together, they melded the ideas of the republic like no other two men could.

When Franklin returned to Philadelphia from his European post in September 1785, he was seventy-nine years old. He had earned a retirement from public life but within days of his arrival he helped quiet the factionalism of Pennsylvania under his leadership. The elder statesman was quickly elected to the state's executive council and elevated to Pennsylvania's presidency by a joint vote of the state assembly and executive council as provided by the Pennsylvania constitution. Washington observed from Mount Vernon:

> He has again embarked on a troubled Ocean; I am persuaded with the best designs, but I wish his purposes may be answered which, undoubtedly are to reconcile the jarring interests of the State. If he should succeed, fresh laurels will crown his brow; but it is to be feared that the task is too great for human wisdom to accomplish.

Franklin was twice reelected to the state's presidency; service beyond the third term he secured in 1787 was prevented by a term limit. Franklin's tenure as the state's president spanned the years the young nation floundered with the Articles of Confederation. Regardless of the country's economic woes and an inability to effectively address public finance under the Articles, Pennsylvania fared better than most states. Despite the relative measure of stability, Franklin needed little persuasion to endorse the idea of a conversation aimed at addressing the faults of the Articles of Confederation.

Virginia was first to call for the convention on December 1, 1786. Edmund Randolph, Virginia's governor, quickly sent Franklin two letters, each lobbying for the participation of Pennsylvania in the convention. Franklin needed little convincing. On December 21 he sent a communication to the Pennsylvania Assembly for the appointment of seven commissioners to the convention. The assembly approved a bill to do just that the next day and Randolph was advised by Franklin that the Pennsylvania commissioners would join the convention at its scheduled opening in May 1787.

The stage was set. Franklin and Washington would spend four long months in Philadelphia during the summer of 1787, all in an effort to establish a government strong enough to ensure order and commerce and thoughtful enough to protect the liberty of its citizens. Washington's welcome to Philadelphia was followed by a dinner party thrown by Franklin at his home on May 16, two days after the convention's formal start. The dinner was attended by delegates from Pennsylvania and Virginia. They enjoyed good food and liquor, something Franklin was prone to use as a tool to promote far-reaching conversations. The dinner was more than a social occasion. The convention had yet to gain a quorum, something that wouldn't happen until May 25, but the dinner served to create the semblance of a plan for going forward.

Once a quorum was in attendance the convention debated, mostly in secret, the nature of new organs of government. Early on, the convention scrapped the idea of revising the Articles of Confederation for a new form of government. One of the critical issues involved an executive branch. Franklin opposed a single executive, having had the less-than-happy experience with the British monarchy. Franklin favored a small council with a rotation of newly elected members. Hamilton argued for a single chief executive. In the end a compromise was reached that blended both concepts. The chief executive would be a single person but subject to election for a term of four years.

The more troublesome question concerned the legislative representation of the states. Again, there were two essential plans that were in opposition. Edmund Randolph championed the Virginia plan, which determined legislature representation by population. The smaller states favored what was known as the New Jersey Plan, a proposal that provided each state equal representation in Congress. The debate between the large states benefited by the Virginian Plan and the small states was heated. The convention itself was threatened by the discord and the summer heat.

The stalemate was broken by Franklin when he proposed a middle path, ultimately to be remembered as the Great Compromise. Franklin introduced a second branch of government. Unlike the House of Representatives, where representation would be established by population, each state would enjoy an equal two legislators in the Senate, the additional branch of government Franklin recommended. Franklin's wisdom and prestige saved the convention and with it the hope of a new and effective form of republican government.

There were other issues to resolve, notably matters attendant to the scourge of the new nation, slavery. Another essential compromise, the treatment of slaves for the purposes of representation in Congress, was resolved by the infamous Three-fifths Clause. In what might constitute the greatest hypocrisy of American government, slaves legally constituting property were to be considered three fifths of a person for the purpose of determining representation in Congress. If that was necessary to win the acceptance of the southern states for the constitution, the new plan of government was less than perfect as Franklin expressly noted.

Franklin's opposition to the slave trade was the earliest manifestation of a philosophy that came to understand the evil of slavery. The slave trade and all the horrors attendant to the kidnapping of Africans followed by a transatlantic crossing that constituted nothing short of hell on earth registered two objections from Franklin. Not only was the practice heinous but it was sponsored, supported, and profited on by the British imperial system. Some colonies sought to reject the trade years before independence, but the British left no choice but to participate. As Franklin grew to understand the evils of British imperialism, the slave trade was a natural part of his indictment of that system.

Franklin's views on slavery show a clear evolution. Before his full conversion to the cause of abolition, he kept two slaves as house servants. Franklin came to understand that the fundamental underpinnings of the American republic could not easily coexist with slavery. If the American republic incorporated liberty as an essential virtue, how could the new government succeed along with slavery? By the mid-1780s, Franklin understood that slavery had to be abolished. By contrast, Jefferson saw the problem as akin to holding a wolf by the ears—you couldn't hold on to it and you can't let it go. With the approval of Franklin, Jefferson condemned the British for establishing and conducting the slave trade in the grievances section of the Declaration of Independence. The southern colonies would not hear of it, so the grievance was deleted. The constitution also reflected the same power of the southern interests.

By the time of the Constitution Convention, Franklin was an abolitionist. He joined America's first abolitionist society, "The Society for Promoting the Abolition of Slavery and the Relief of Negroes," founded by Quakers in 1775, upon his return from France in 1785. In 1787, the same year the Constitutional Convention convened, Franklin became the Society's president. Franklin understood the document that emerged from the 1787 convention was flawed but he accepted it as a political expedient. His departing speech at the convention, delivered by James Wilson, a better orator than the aging Franklin, sums up the reality of government when Franklin signed his name to the new constitution: "I agree to this constitution with all its faults, if they are such; because I think a general government necessary for us...Thus, I consent, sir, to this constitution, because I expect no better, and because I am not sure that it is not the best."

After the installation of the three branches of the new national government, Franklin turned his attention to abolition, more pointedly during his last days. On February 3, 1798, Franklin petitioned the First Congress, then meeting in New York City, to address the slavery question.

> That mankind are all formed by the same Almighty being, alike objects of his Care & equally designed for the Enjoyment of Happiness the Christian Religion teaches us to believe & the Political Creed of America fully coincides with the Position. Your Memorialists, particularly engaged in attending to the Distresses arising from

Slavery, believe it their indispensable Duty to present this Subject to your notice. They have observed with great Satisfaction that many important & salutary Powers are vested in you for "promoting the Welfare & Securing the blessings of liberty to the "People of the United States." And as they conceive, that these blessings of liberty to the "People of the United States." And as they conceive, that these blessings ought rightfully to be administered, without distinction of Colour, to all descriptions of People, so they indulge themselves in the pleasing expectation, that nothing, which can be done for the relive of the unhappy objects of their care, will be either omitted or delayed.

From a persuasion that equal liberty was originally the Portion, It is still the Birthright of all men, & influenced by the strong ties of Humanity & the Principles of their Institution, your Memorialists conceive themselves bound to use all justifiable endeavours to loosen the bound of Slavery and promote a general Enjoyment of the blessings of Freedom. Under these Impressions they earnestly entreat your serious attention to the Subject of Slavery, that you will be pleased to countenance the Restoration of liberty to those unhappy Men, who alone, in this land of Freedom, are degraded into perpetual Bondage, and who, amidst the general Joy of surrounding Freeman, are groaning in Servile Subjection, that you will devise.

The petition was entered on the record in the House on February 12 and the Senate three days later. Franklin's initiative met with violent opposition by pro-slavery legislators in both Houses of Congress. The Senate never took action on the petition. The House sent it to committee. The committee report was returned on March 5, 1790, and it was determined to violate the terms of the constitution since the slave trade was protected by that document until at least 1808 and presumably the holding of slaves in perpetuity. The petition was then tabled, consigned to the dustbin of history. Franklin himself passed from this mortal coil only a few weeks after his petition, on April 17, 1790, at age eighty-four. The last great act of his long and illustrious life was not accomplished. One can only wonder just what the future of slavery would have been if Franklin had been fifty-four in 1790 and not eighty-four.

Epilogue

Possessed of unending vision and boundless energy, both Benjamin Franklin and Walt Disney never gave up on improving the world around them. To their dying breath, each man dared to dream, to imagine a better way. There are few, if any, Americans who have accomplished such a vast number of improvements to the human condition. Just as rare are individuals, who realize so much of what they envision for the future.

There have always been dreamers, people creative enough to see the world in a different way and bold enough to say it. Not all dreamers, however, are doers. Special are those innovators who not only understand us but can chart a course and take us all along the way with them. Franklin and Disney, more than any other quality they possessed, understood just who their fellow Americans were. They understood human nature and more particularly the American psyche better than just about any American at any time in our history. That is remarkable by itself, but both men were so much more.

They each had an unquenchable thirst to share what they understood so well with us. They wanted us to see what they saw, to feel what they felt and to triumph together. Theirs was not a quest based on profit, revenue, or greed. If their missions were self-serving, it was only to foster their own vanity—fashion a legacy for themselves. And after all, what harm does a desire for legacy by us mere mortals occasion if the byproduct is good for our fellow human beings? Franklin was always willing to view a topic and himself with an open mind. He recognized the impulse to fashion a reputation for himself and summed it up quite eloquently in his famous quote on human vanity.

Two sons of humble beginnings, two men with inauspicious starts, both Franklin and Disney rose above their circumstances in ways that serve as the shining examples of the American promise so long ingrained as a part of our country's fundamental creed. They each took the American promise to a different place and by exercising their opportunities like few have, they defined and redefined just who we are as Americans. We are better off for how they lived, for the culture they created and recreated.

Disney honored the American experience, our history and heritage. His patriotism, well established in his craft, would surprise no one. Though he never saw the opening of EPCOT, it was his last dream, the unfinished vision he died with. EPCOT opened in 1982, sixteen years after Walt's death. The World Showcase, a collection of pavilions hosted by eleven nations, is anchored by a host pavilion called the American Adventure. Inside the stately colonial building is a theatre featuring a seventy-two-foot panoramic screen and thirty-five audio-animatronic figures from American history. Two of the figures are your hosts for an inspiring trip through American history.

Those hosts are none other than Benjamin Franklin and America's prominent entertainer before the birth of the film industry, Mark Twain.

Disney and Franklin would have approved of the first sentences spoken by the Franklin figure:

> America did not exist. Four centuries of work, of bloodshed, of loneliness and fear created this land. We built America and the process made us Americans – a new breed, rooted in all races, stained and tinted with all colors, a seeming ethnic anarchy. Then in a little time, we become more alike than we were different – a new society; not great, but fitted by our very faults for greatness.

The profound Franklin and Twain banter back and forth over whether those words of a great statesman belonged to Twain. Franklin quickly points out the prose was not Twain's but was attributed to John Steinbeck, a twentieth-century American writer.

Nevertheless, Franklin and Disney would have approved of the pragmatic optimism. They were keenly aware of America's shortcomings, Franklin as the architect of compromises that were essential to the country's founding and Disney as one who understood the rough-and-tumble of a business world that more than once created hurdles difficult to clear. Despite those experiences, each man maintained a stubborn optimism. They believed America was different and they believed the opportunity promised by this land could change the world.

And change the world they did. It is for us to enjoy the fruits of what they sowed but more importantly, we must understand that their dreaming, daring, and doing remains a challenge for all generations. The American culture will endure, always with a gracious nod to Franklin and Disney, men who left a legacy as rich as our national heritage.

❧

Portrait of Benjamin Franklin made by artist
Joseph-Siffred Duplessis in 1783,
from the collection of the New York Public Library.

Portrait of Benjamin Franklin made by artist David Martin in 1767. The bust in the portrait is of Isaac Newton. The document in Franklin's hands is not a treaty or act but a deed belonging to William Alexander of Edinburgh, who commissioned the 50 x 40 oil painting, from the Philadelphia Academy of Fine Arts.

An engraving of Benjamin Franklin's famous kite-flying experiment in September 1752, from Les merveilles de la science, ou Description Populaire des inventions modernes, 1867, by Louis Figuier, fig. 333, Houghton Library, Harvard University.

The drafting of the Declaration of Independence, from the Philadelphia Museum of Art.

"The signing of the Constitution," as portrayed in the 1925 painting Foundation of American Government by John Henry Hintermeister. Washington, sitting, watches Gouverneur Morris sign while Franklin stands to the rear.

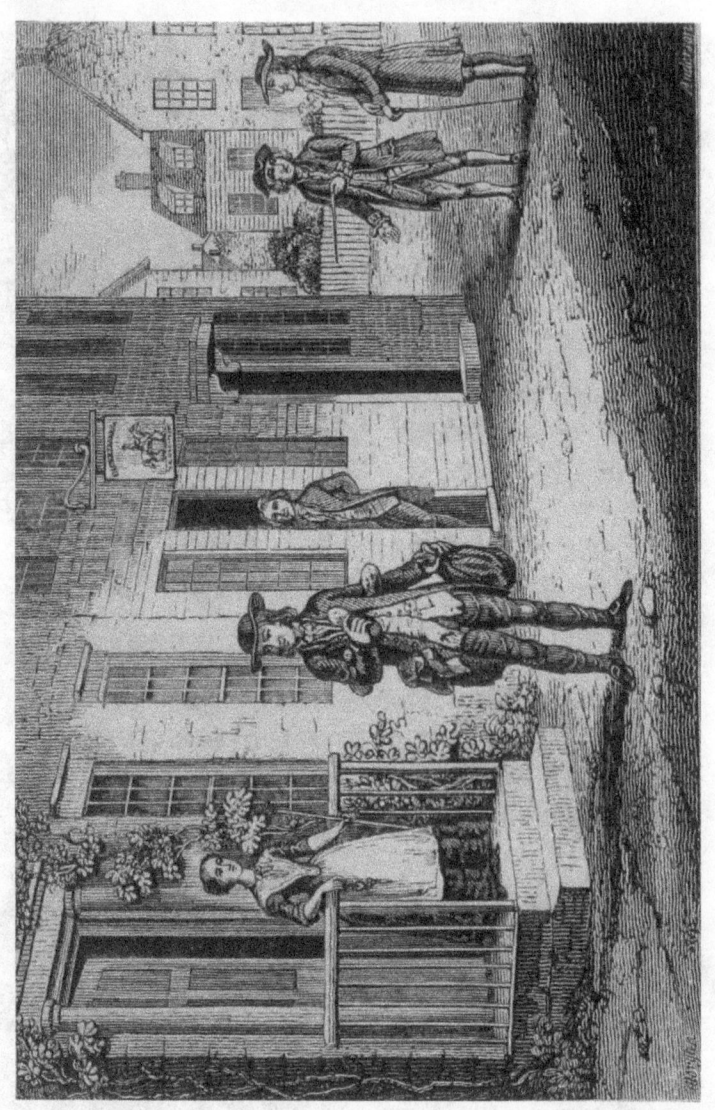

Franklin, newly arrived in Philadelphia, makes his way up Market Street with rolls he purchased from his meager savings. In the doorway is his future wife, Ms. Read. Franklin lamented that he made a most "awkward and ridiculous appearance." From *The Life of Benjamin Franklin,* O. L. Hurley and Alexander Anderson, 1848. Library of Congress Collection.

Entrance to Disneyland in California, 1955 by photographer Carol Highsmith.

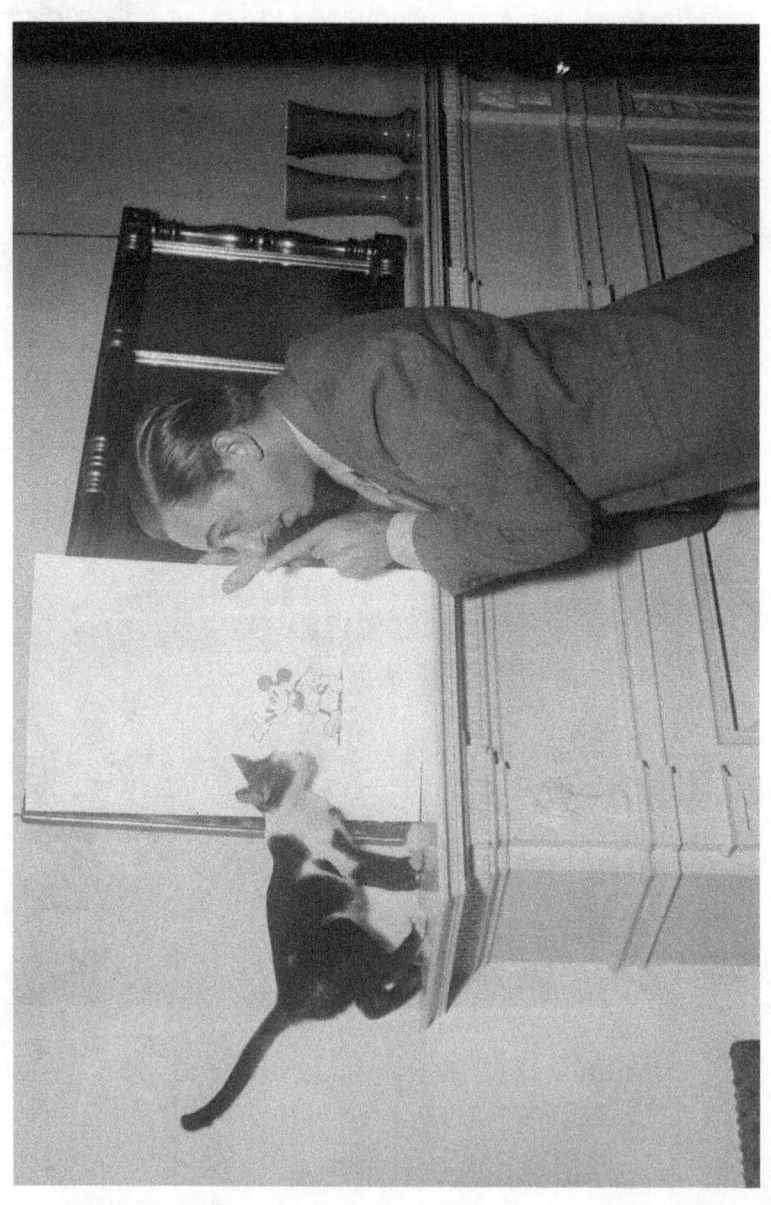

A playful Walt Disney entertains a cat with an illustration of Mickey Mouse in the background. The photo was taken by Harris & Ewing Photographer in 1931.

"Steamboat Willie"
from the 1928 short that changed
animation forever.

The first stamp issued by the US Postal Service commemorating Walt Disney. The six-cent first-class rate stamp debuted in 1968 and was designed by Disney artists.

Endnotes

Introduction

Franklin had sixteen brothers: H.W. Brands, *The First American: The Life and Times of Benjamin Franklin* (New York, NY: Doubleday, 2000), 15.

They both left home at age seventeen: H.W. Brands, *The First American*, 34.

They both left home at, or near, age seventeen: Bob Thomas, *Walt Disney* (New York, NY: Hyperion, 1976), 47.

Chapter 1

Oxford University awarded: Walter Isaacson, *Benjamin Franklin: An American Life* (New York, NY: Simon & Schuster, 2003), 202.

William's appointment as Royal Governor: H.W. Brands, *The First American: The Life and Times of Benjamin Franklin* (New York, NY: Doubleday, 2000), 327.

First and foremost a Briton: H.W. Brands, *The First American*, 308.

The Pennsylvania Assembly appointed him: Walter Isaacson, *Benjamin Franklin*, 217.

Massachusetts Colonial Assembly dated November 6, 1770: To Benjamin Franklin from the Massachusetts House of Representatives, 6 November 1770, *Founders Online, National Archives,* https://founders.archieves.gov/documents/Franklin/01-17-02-0165 (accessed January 23, 2023).

The petition was received by Franklin: H.W. Brands, *The First American*, 451.

The second event: From Benjamin Franklin to Thomas Cushing, 2 December 1772, *Founders Online, National Archives,* https://founders.archieves.gov/documents/Franklin/01-19-02-0267 (accessed January 23, 2023).

Lord President of the Privy Council, Earl Gower, requested: H.W. Brands, *The First American*, 468.

While Bailyn admits his opinion is conjectural: Bailyn gives attribution to and thanks G. B. Warden, assistant editor of *The Papers of Benjamin Franklin* for, "allowing me to see his progress report" through 1972 on the identity of the person the Papers later identify as "X."

Temple's solitary access: H.W. Brands, *The First American*, 466.

Bell asserts that an anonymous: Jeremy John Bell, *The Mystery of the Hutchinson Letters,* https://vimeo.com/859430520 (accessed January 2023).

Various reasons have been advanced: The Final Hearing before the Privy Council Committee for Plantation Affairs on the Petition from the Massachusetts House of Representatives for the Removal of Hutchinson and Oliver, 29 January 1774, *Founders Online, National Archives,* https://founders.archieves.gov/documents/Franklin/01-21-02-0018 (accessed January 30, 2023).

Franklin also advised Cushing: The Final Hearing before the Privy Council Committee for Plantation Affairs on the Petition from the Massachusetts House of

Representatives for the Removal of Hutchinson and Oliver, 29 January 1774, *Founders Online, National Archives,* https://founders.archieves.gov/documents/Franklin (accessed January 30, 2023).

The supplying of these letters without their eventual publication: Cushing requested that Franklin make copies of the letters on at least two occasions by correspondence dated March 24, 1773 and April 20, 1773. In his letter to Franklin dated June 14, 1773, Cushing informed Franklin that the original letters and copies were in possession of John Hancock, who had laid both before the House to be publicly compared. (See *Papers of B.F.,* V. 20, p. 123, N9 and p. 237).

Chapter 2

Franklin's involvement in obtaining and publishing the Hutchinson letters: In a letter addressed to Speaker Cushing but intended for the Massachusetts House dated July 7, 1773, Franklin exposed his role in the theft of the Hutchinson letters. While the letter was not read before the House until January 1774, its contents became known long before to many including Governor Hutchinson himself. Hutchinson sent news of the letter to Lord Dartmouth on October 19, 1773, but did not include a copy of Franklin's letter for purposes not unlike Franklin's reasoning in his letter to Samuel Cooper of July 1773 (see *Papers of B.F.,* V. 20, p. 277, including N. 10).

Temple challenged Whatley to a duel: H.W. Brands, *The First American: The Life and Times of Benjamin Franklin* (New York, NY: Doubleday, 2000), 466.

First Summons to the Privy Council: H.W. Brands, *The First American*, 467.

On January 22, 1774, the St. James Chronicle published the first news of the Tea Party in London, Thomas Fleming, *Liberty! – The American Revolution*, (New York; NY, 1997), 81.

These are letters which Dr. Franklin treats: The Final Hearing before the Privy Council Committee for Plantation Affairs on the Petition from the Massachusetts House of Representatives for the Removal of Hutchinson and Oliver, 29 January 1774, *Founders Online, National Archives,* https://founders.archieves.gov/documents/Franklin (accessed January 30, 2023).

Throughout Franklin remained emotionless: H.W. Brands, *The First American*, 474.

The Doctor was dressed in a full dress suit: Walter Isaacson, *Benjamin Franklin: An American Life* (New York, NY: Simon & Schuster, 2003), 277.

Chapter 3

Television attracted Walt's attention: Wade Sampson, The First Disney Television Christmas, https://www.mouseplanet.com/8605/The_First-Disney_Television_Christmas (accessed February 4, 2023).

In May 1939: Wade Sampson, The First Disney Television Christmas, https://www.mouseplanet.com/The_First-Disney_Television_Christmas (accessed February 4, 2023).

Endnotes

By 1944 RCA was entreating Walt Disney: Wade Sampson, The First Disney Television Christmas, https://www.mouseplanet.com/8605/The_First-Disney_Television_Christmas (accessed February 4, 2023).

The Decision of Disney Studios: Neal Gabler, *Walt Disney: The Triumph of American Imagination,* (New York, NY: Vintage Books, 2006), 503.

Walt was a bit concerned: Wade Sampson, The First Disney Television Christmas, https://www.mouseplanet.com/The_First-Disney_Television_Christmas (accessed February 4, 2023).

Walt was convinced and he let his stockholders in on his views: Wade Sampson, The First Disney Television Christmas, https://www.mouseplanet.com/The_First-Disney_Television_Christmas (accessed February 4, 2023).

Unlike most studio executives: Neal Gabler, *Walt Disney,* 503.

Chapter 4

While most scholars do not believe that Franklin: "What did America's founding fathers know about mental illness," https://www.cugmph.org/five-on-friday-posts/what-did-americas-founding-fathers-know-about-mental-illness/ (accessed February 11, 2023).

Disney biographer Neal Gabler: Neal Gabler, *Walt Disney: The Triumph of American Imagination,* (New York, NY: Vintage Books, 2006), 166.

The flashpoint of his breakdown: Neal Gabler, *Walt Disney,* 163.

The immediate crisis: Neal Gabler, *Walt Disney*, 104.

Case in point, Elias bought a paper route: Bob Thomas, *Walt Disney* (New York, NY: Hyperion, 1976), 33.

When he retired, Walt announced he envied Herbert's life: Neal Gabler, *Walt Disney*, 440.

Elias and Flora's second son Raymond was originally named Walter: Neal Gabler, *Walt Disney*, 9.

In 1937 Walt and Ray bought their parents a home: Neal Gabler, *Walt Disney*, 304.

Striking Disney Workers: *The Disney Strike, 1941;* https://animationguild.org/about-the-guild/disney-strike-1941/ (accessed March 10, 2023).

Though Marceline passed into memory: "The Magic of Marceline," https://d23.com/the-magic-of-marceline/ (accessed February 19, 2024).

Chapter 5

The bookish inclination: L. Jesse Lemisch, ed., *Benjamin Franklin, The Autobiographer and Other Writings*, (New York, NY: Signet Classic, 1961),. 26.

Ben's indenture bound him: L. Jesse Lemisch, ed., *Benjamin Franklin, The Autobiographer*, 27.

Franklin recounted his poor treatment: L. Jesse Lemisch, ed., *Benjamin Franklin, The Autobiographer*, 33.

Before long James got himself in a bit of a bind: H.W. Brands, The First American: *The Life and Times of Benjamin Franklin* (New York, NY: Doubleday, 2000), 30.

Josiah Franklin sided with James: L. Jesse Lemisch, ed., *Benjamin Franklin, The Autobiographer*, 35.

In Chicago Walt enrolled as a freshman at McKinley: Neal Gabler, *Walt Disney: The Triumph of American Imagination,* (New York, NY: Vintage Books, 2006), 32.

The war in Germany preoccupied Americans: Bob Thomas, *Walt Disney* (New York, NY: Hyperion, 1976), 45-46.

Chapter 6

I offered my services: L. Jesse Lemisch, ed., *Benjamin Franklin, The Autobiographer and Other Writings,* (New York, NY: Signet Classic, 1961), 35.

Philadelphia was a hundred miles further: L. Jesse Lemisch, ed., *Benjamin Franklin, The Autobiographer,* 35.

Ever the craftsman: L. Jesse Lemisch, ed., *Benjamin Franklin, The Autobiographer,* 36.

The next leg of Franklin's trip: L. Jesse Lemisch, ed., *Benjamin Franklin, The Autobiographer,* 37.

Franklin's first steps in the city: L. Jesse Lemisch, ed., *Benjamin Franklin, The Autobiographer,* 38.

Franklin's appetite led him to a bakery: L. Jesse Lemisch, ed., *Benjamin Franklin, The Autobiographer,* 39.

While the printing trade: L. Jesse Lemisch, ed., *Benjamin Franklin, The Autobiographer,* 41.

Soon Franklin's brother-in-law Robert Holmes: L. Jesse Lemisch, ed., *Benjamin Franklin, The Autobiographer,* 42.

In late 1724, Governor Keith: L. Jesse Lemisch, ed., *Benjamin Franklin, The Autobiographer,* 54.

When Walt returned from France: Bob Thomas, *Walt Disney* (New York, NY: Hyperion, 1976), 55.

While working at the film ad company: Bob Thomas, *Walt Disney*, 57.

On May 18, 1921, he filed certificate: Missouri Secretary of State File 39844.

Laugh-O-Gram Films consisted: Neal Gabler, *Walt Disney: The Triumph of American Imagination*, (New York, NY: Vintage Books, 2006), 63.

The job involved producing an educational film: Neal Gabler, *Walt Disney*, 69.

In July of 1923 Laugh-O-Gram declared bankruptcy: Bob Thomas, *Walt Disney*, 66.

In 1923, a much more modest effect: Bob Thomas, *Walt Disney*, 71.

Toiled at his Laugh-O-Gram desk: Bob Thomas, *Walt Disney*, 112.

Chapter 7

Franklin left London on July 23, 1726: H.W. Brands, *The First American: The Life and Times of Benjamin Franklin* (New York, NY: Doubleday, 2000), 83.

Franklin and Denham sailed: L. Jesse Lemisch, ed., *Benjamin Franklin, The Autobiographer and Other Writings*, (New York, NY: Signet Classic, 1961), 63.

For the incidents of the voyage: L. Jesse Lemisch, ed., *Benjamin Franklin, The Autobiographer*, 64.

The shop-keeping business was not entirely agreeable: L. Jesse Lemisch, ed., *Benjamin Franklin, The Autobiographer*, 65.

It didn't take Franklin long: L. Jesse Lemisch, ed., *Benjamin Franklin, The Autobiographer*, 65.

As things progressed: L. Jesse Lemisch, ed., *Benjamin Franklin, The Autobiographer*, 67.

In the last months of 1727: L. Jesse Lemisch, ed., *Benjamin Franklin, The Autobiographer*, 68.

The year 1728, exactly two centuries: L. Jesse Lemisch, ed., *Benjamin Franklin, The Autobiographer*, 70.

In the span of less than four years: H.W. Brands, *The First American*, 103.

In the end, Hugh Meredith faced reality: L. Jesse Lemisch, ed., *Benjamin Franklin, The Autobiographer*, 76.

When Franklin ended one partnership in 1730: L. Jesse Lemisch, ed., *Benjamin Franklin, The Autobiographer*, 81.

Franklin's first publication of Poor Richard's Almanac: L. Jesse Lemisch, ed., *Benjamin Franklin, The Autobiographer*, 107.

Chapter 8

In July 1923, Walt stood on the platform: Neal Gabler, *Walt Disney: The Triumph of American Imagination*, (New York, NY: Vintage Books, 2006), 74.

He looked like the devil: Neal Gabler, *Walt Disney*, 77.

For Christ sake, don't you get TB: Roy himself was out west recovering from the disease. He left Arizona for California, thinking he had little time left and that was where he wanted to spend his remaining days.

Walt let a room from his uncle Robert Disney: Neal Gabler, *Walt Disney*, 78.

On October 15, 1923, Winkler sent: Bob Thomas, *Walt Disney* (New York, NY: Hyperion, 1976), 72, 73.

In December, the brothers took a new apartment: Neal Gabler, *Walt Disney*, 83.

The series would be known as the Alice Comedies: Bob Thomas, *Walt Disney*, 76.

Business wasn't the only thing the Disney Bros.: Neal Gabler, *Walt Disney*, 92.

Despite a pledge he wouldn't get married: Neal Gabler, *Walt Disney*, 95.

The partners were so confident: Neal Gabler, *Walt Disney*, 96.

I'm going to hang a large neon sign: Jack Kinney, *Walt Disney and Other Animated Characters: An Unauthorized Account of the Early Years at Disney's*, (New York: Harmony Books, 1988), 198.

By March 1927, Mintz signed a contract: *Motion Picture World*, March 12, 1927.

Soon after, the brothers built modest homes: Neal Gabler, *Walt Disney*, 104.

There would be no negotiating the price: Neal Gabler, *Walt Disney*, 109.

As legend has it: Walt Disney, Autobiography (unpublished manuscript), 1934, Walt Disney Archives.

Walt was running low on finances: Neal Gabler, *Walt Disney*, 125.

Harry Reichenbach was the manager: Neal Gabler, *Walt Disney*, 126.

Steamboat Willie: Bob Thomas, *Walt Disney*, 96.

Chapter 9

Franklin invented a new wat to heat a home: https://www.history.org/franklin/science/stove.htm#google_vignette (accessed March 3, 2023).

In order of time I should have mentioned: L. Jesse Lemisch, ed., *Benjamin Franklin, The Autobiographer and Other Writings*, (New York, NY: Signet Classic, 1961), 128.

One of Disney's animators, Ken Anderson: Bob Thomas, *Walt Disney* (New York, NY: Hyperion, 1976), 130.

By mid-1938, the Disney Studio employed 500: Neal Gabler, *Walt Disney: The Triumph of American Imagination*, (New York, NY: Vintage Books, 2006), 236.

As the film progressed, the deadline of Christmas 1937: Neal Gabler, *Walt Disney*, 271.

Snow White premiered: Frank S. Nugent, "The Music Hall Presents Walt Disney's Delightful Fantasy, 'Snow White and the Seven Dwarfs," *The New York Times*, January 14, 1938, 21.

Snow White earned $8 million dollars: Bob Thomas, *Walt Disney,* 143.

Beyond all accolades: https://www.mouseplanet.com/13155/The_education_of_Walt_Disney# (accessed March 8, 2023).

Chapter 10

Franklin was acquainted by Dr. Spence: L. Jesse Lemisch, ed., *Benjamin Franklin, The Autobiographer and Other Writings,* (New York, NY: Signet Classic, 1961), 164.

Soon after my return to Philadelphia: L. Jesse Lemisch, ed., *Benjamin Franklin, The Autobiographer,* 104.

Just two days before Christmas Day in 1750: *APS News* (Advanced Physics), December 2006 (Volume 15, Number 11).

Cave it seems, judged rightly: L. Jesse Lemisch, ed., *Benjamin Franklin, The Autobiographer,* 165.

The book, experiments and observations on electricity made at Philadelphia in America: H.W. Brands, *The First American: The Life and Times of Benjamin Franklin* (New York, NY: Doubleday, 2000), 273.

Franklin's theory found quick criticism in France as well: H.W. Brands, *The First American,* 190.

Franklin relates the wholesale shift: L. Jesse Lemisch, ed., *Benjamin Franklin, The Autobiographer,* 166.

Five months subsequent to the Dalibard experiment: https://fi.edu/en/science-and-education/benjamin-franklin/kite-key-experiement (accessed March 9, 2023).

Franklin's kite experiment: L. Jesse Lemisch, ed., *Benjamin Franklin, The Autobiographer,* 107.

Chapter 11

One critic praised *Dumbo*: Neal Gabler, Walt Disney: *The Triumph of American Imagination,* (New York, NY: Vintage Books, 2006), Pg. 381.

An article written in *TIME*: *TIME*'s plans to put *Dumbo* on the cover of the December 29 issue changed after the December 7 attack on Pearl Harbor. Instead, they included a short article about *Dumbo* in the December 15 issue, "framing him as a welcome distraction and source of comfort for a country at war." Andrew R. Chow, "How Dumbo almost Ended Up on the Cover of *TIME*," *TIME Magazine,* March 29, 2019, https://time.com/5557249/dumbo-time-cover-1941/L.

500 U.S. Amry troops: Bob Thomas, *Walt Disney* (New York, NY: Hyperion, 1976), 175.

Disney's transformation came along: Richard Snow, *Disney's Land* (New York, NY: Scribner, 2019), 37.

Hazel George knew Walt's innermost thoughts: https://disney.fandom.com/wiki/Hazel_George (accessed March 11, 2023).

A crossroad came: Bob Thomas, *Walt Disney,* 214.

Walt set his Lionel train up: Bob Thomas, *Walt Disney,* 213.

The couple found a suitable lot: Bob Thomas, *Walt Disney,* 215.

Walt's merriment and sense of whimsey: "Walt Disney, 65, Dies on Coast; Founded an Empire Based on a Mouse," *The New York Times*, December 16, 1966.

Chapter 12

Franklin was nominated to serve in the Pennsylvania Assembly: Walter Isaacson, *Benjamin Franklin: An American Life* (New York, NY: Simon & Schuster, 2003), 153.

I conceived my becoming a member: H.W. Brands, *The First American: The Life and Times of Benjamin Franklin* (New York, NY: Doubleday, 2000), 209.

However mischievous those creatures: H.W. Brands, *The First American*, 206.

The contribution to the crime problems: H.W. Brands, *The First American*, 219.

The Carlisle Treaty: Walter Isaacson, *Benjamin Franklin*, 156.

As those people are extremely apt to get drunk: L. Jesse Lemisch, ed., *Benjamin Franklin, The Autobiographer and Other Writings*, (New York, NY: Signet Classic, 1961), 132.

In the 1754 war with France: L. Jesse Lemisch, ed., *Benjamin Franklin, The Autobiographer*, 140.

He also created what is generally credited: https://www.digitalhistory.uh.edu/active_learning/explorations/revolution/cartoon4.cfm (accessed March 16, 2023).

The Albany Congress began on June 19: https://founders.archives.gov/documents/Franklin/01-05-02-0096 (accessed March 16, 2023).

Chapter 13

Disneyland doesn't have a precise birthdate: Neal Gabler, *Walt Disney: The Triumph of American Imagination*, (New York, NY: Vintage Books, 2006), 483.

The cleanliness and quality of food offerings at Tivoli: Bob Thomas, *Walt Disney* (New York, NY: Hyperion, 1976), 24.

In December of 1952: Neal Gabler, *Walt Disney*, 493.

With the financial security of his deal: Bob Thomas, *Walt Disney*, 242.

Art Directors Dick Irvine and: Neal Gabler, *Walt Disney*, 492-493.

Postwar America: https://www.loc.gov/classroom-materials/united-states-history-primary-source-timeline/post-war-united-states-1945/overview (accessed March 30, 2023).

The answer came suddenly: Bob Thomas, *Walt Disney*, 244.

Walt continued his plea: Bob Thomas, *Walt Disney*, 245.

Look, Herbie, my brother Roy: Bob Thomas, *Walt Disney*, 246.

The deadline was Monday morning: Neal Gabler, *Walt Disney*, 507.

The idea of Disneyland is a simple one: Bob Thomas, *Walt Disney*, 246.

It will be just another Coney Island: Richard Snow, *Disney's Land* (New York, NY: Scribner, 2019), 98.

I want your television show but: Richard Snow, *Disney's Land*, 99.

Roy Disney secured from ABC: Bob Thomas, *Walt Disney*, 249.

If anyone doubled the promise: Neal Gabler, *Walt Disney*, 514.

The frenzy over Davy Crockett: Neal Gabler, *Walt Disney*, 518.

There were more than a few hiccups: https://abc7/amp/disneyland-birthday-opening-day-66-when-did-open/1429121 (accessed March 30, 2023).

Chapter 14

The French and Indian War: H.W. Brands, *The First American: The Life and Times of Benjamin Franklin* (New York, NY: Doubleday, 2000), 285.

The realities nearly a century later: https://www.fpri.org/article/2020/07/william-penn-benjamin-franklin-and-the-american-founding-the-philadelphia-factor-2/.

The colony's governor was controlled: https://www.mountvernon.org/library/digitalhistory/digital-encyclopedia/article/benjamin-franklin-in-london/.

Franklin's meetings with the Penns: Walter Isaacson, *Benjamin Franklin: An American Life* (New York, NY: Simon & Schuster, 2003), 302.

The Penn's did what wealthy people have long done: H.W. Brands, *The First American*, 314.

The council exempted much of their land: https://allthingsliberty.com/2017/09/benjamin-franklins-mission-london-1757-1762/.

New at the Privy Council's decree: https://allthingsliberty.com/2017/09/benjamin-franklins-mission-london-1757-1762/.

Most people dislike vanity in others: L. Jesse Lemisch, ed., *Benjamin Franklin, The Autobiographer and Other Writings,* (New York, NY: Signet Classic, 1961), 17.

Notably his social circle included: H.W. Brands, *The First American*, 320.

Franklin's second stay in London: https://www.smithsonianmag.com/history/ben-franklin-was-one-fifth-revolutionary-four-fifths-london-intellectual-180958256/.

Franklin's return to Philadelphia: H.W. Brands, *The First American*, 361.

The law was conceived by Grenville: Edmund S. Morgan and Helen M. Morgan, *The Stamp Act Crisis: Prologue to Revolution* (New York, NY 1902), 89-91.

In the wake of the passage of the act: H.W. Brands, *The First American*, 363.

The reaction in the colonies to the Stamp Act: Walter Isaacson, *Benjamin Franklin*, 224-225.

In Philadelphia, Hughes and Deborah: Walter Isaacson, *Benjamin Franklin*, 224.

"George III dismissed Grenville":
https://www.nps.gov/articles/000/anger-and-opposition-to-the-stamp-act.htm.

Franklin's testimony was persuasive: H.W. Brands, *The First American,* 374.

The Declaratory Act, which confirmed Parliament's plenary authority: Edmund S. Morgan and Helen M. Morgan, *The Stamp Act Crisis,* 377.

Chapter 15

Lillian and Walt's thirtieth: Bob Thomas, *Walt Disney* (New York, NY: Hyperion, 1976), 277.

Four days later: Bob Thomas, *Walt Disney,* 274.

The Disneyland television series:
https://ctva.biz/US/Anthology/Walt/Disney_02_(1955-56).htm (accessed March 23, 2023).

On October 3, 1955: Bob Thomas, *Walt Disney,* 275.

Famously Russian Premier: Neal Gabler, *Walt Disney: The Triumph of American Imagination,* (New York, NY: Vintage Books, 2006), 565.

The revenue of Walt Disney Productions: Bob Thomas, *Walt Disney,* 286.

RCA had been manufacturing:
https://wired.com/2008/03/dayintech-0325/ (accessed April 1, 2023).

On September 24, 1961:
https://en.m.wikipedia.org/wiki/Disney_Anthology_television_series (accessed April 2, 2023).

One year before Walt's death: https://en.m.wikipedia.org/wiki/Mary_Poppins_(book_series) (accessed April 2, 2023).

The movie premiered: Bob Thomas, *Walt Disney*, 322.

The movie drew widespread critical acclaim: James Powers, Review of *Mary Poppins*, *The Hollywood Reporter*, August 27, 1964.

Variety chimed in: Whitney Williams, "Film Review: Mary Poppins," *Variety*, December 31, 1963 (article appeared before the film was released in August 1964).

The film's quality: Bob Thomas, *Walt Disney*, 322.

***Mary Poppins* garnered thirteen:** Neal Gabler, *Walt Disney*, 600.

Chapter 16

Benjamin Franklin left Philadelphia: https://www.smithsonianmag.com/history/ben-franklin-was-one-fifth-revolutionary-four-fifths-london-intellectual-180958256/.

The British losses numbered 270 killed: H.W. Brands, *The First American: The Life and Times of Benjamin Franklin* (New York, NY: Doubleday, 2000), 496.

When Franklin landed in Philadelphia: Edward J. Larson, *Franklin & Washington: The Founding Partnership* (New York, NY: Harper Collins, 2020), 94.

Washington Arrived in Philadelphia: Edward J. Larson, *Franklin & Washington*, 94.

On June 11, 1776: Calvin D. Linton, ed: *The Bicentennial Almanac* (Nashville, TN: Thomas Nelson Publishers, 1975), 20.

Franklin's most famous edit:
https://www.smithsonianmag.com/history/benjamin-franklin-joins-the-revolution-87199988/.

No American colonist could have:
https://www.smithsonianmag.com/history/benjamin-franklin-joins-the-revolution-87199988/.

On September 26, 1776: Walter Isaacson, *Benjamin Franklin: An American Life* (New York, NY: Simon & Schuster, 2003), 324-325.

Franklin made quite an impression: Stacy Schiff, *A Great Improvisation: Franklin, France, and the Birth of America,* (New York, NY: Henry Holt and Company, 2005), 2.

The French Foreign Minister: Stacy Schiff, *A Great Improvisation,* 204.

Burgoyne's lumbering advance: Calvin D. Linton, ed: *The Bicentennial Almanac,* 23.

For the occasion, Franklin wore: Edward J. Larson, *Franklin & Washington,* 132.

Chapter 17

The new park would likely go east: Aaron H. Golders, *Buying Disney World: The Story of How Florida Swampland Became Walt Disney World,* (Philadelphia, PA: Quaker Scribe Publishing, 2021), 15.

Walt hired a research economist: Aaron H. Golders, *Buying Disney World,* 15.

In 1961, Price divided Florida: Aaron H. Golders, *Buying Disney World,* 20.

In 1960, Walt and his company: https://www.waltdisney.org/blog/look-closer-1964-new-york-worlds-fair.

He had experimented with the concept since: Neal Gabler, *Walt Disney: The Triumph of American Imagination,* (New York, NY: Vintage Books, 2006), 579.

Ford didn't buy Walt's pitch for: https://www.waltdisney.org/blog/look-closer-1964-new-york-worlds-fair.

Another Disney-created pavilion: Neal Gabler, *Walt Disney,* 576.

As the fair drew closer: https://www.waltdisney.org/blog/look-closer-1964-new-york-worlds-fair.

The results of the team's work: Neal Gabler, *Walt Disney,* 580.

The fourth and final pavilion: Neal Gabler, *Walt Disney,* 582.

Fresh from the sober commitment: Karal Ann Marling, *Designing Disney's Theme Parks: The Architecture of Reassurance,* (New York: Flammarion, 1997), 132.

Walt was in New York on April 20, 1964: Aaron H. Golders, *Buying Disney World,* 33.

Results from the fair as well as: Aaron H. Golders, *Buying Disney World,* 20.

Total attendance: Aaron H. Golders, *Buying Disney World,* 22.

Chapter 18

Franklin published his reflections on chess:
https://founders.archives.gov/documents/Franklin/01-29-02-0608.

Franklin had good reason: H.W. Brands, *The First American: The Life and Times of Benjamin Franklin* (New York, NY: Doubleday, 2000), 609.

The British understood: H.W. Brands, *The First American*, 598.

Though Franklin made it clear:
https://history.state.gov/milestones/1776-1783/treaty.

Great Britian had waged a six-year war: H.W. Brands, *The First American*, 602.

The question of a separate peace: H.W. Brands, *The First American*, 615.

Franklin and his fellow commissioners:
https://history.state.gov/milestones/1776-1783/treaty.

Preliminary articles:
https://history.state.gov/milestones/1776-1783/treaty.

Chapter 19

He was tired and looked it: Neal Gabler, *Walt Disney: The Triumph of American Imagination,* (New York, NY: Vintage Books, 2006), 625.

The neck surgery never happened: Neal Gabler, *Walt Disney*, 626.

Walt, who celebrated his sixty-fifth: Neal Gabler, *Walt Disney*, 630.

Walt briefed the crowd: https://www.mouseplanet.com/12125/The_1965_Florida_Press_Conference.

After Walt's death: Aaron H. Golders, *Buying Disney World: The Story of How Florida Swampland Became Walt Disney World,* (Philadelphia, PA: Quaker Scribe Publishing, 2021), 104.

Standing next to Mickey Mouse: https://disneyparks.disney.go.com/blog/2021/10/walt-disney-world-memories-roy-o-disney-dedicates-the-resort/.

Chapter 20

The greatest rumblings: Mark C. Bodanza, *Risk Takers & History Makers: The Story of Leominster* (Leominster, MA: North Hill Press, 2019), 31.

Washington would have a partner: Edward J. Larson, *Franklin & Washington: The Founding Partnership* (New York, NY: Harper Collins, 2020), x.

Once again Franklin was called: H.W. Brands, *The First American: The Life and Times of Benjamin Franklin* (New York, NY: Doubleday, 2000), 672.

Washington arrived in Philadelphia: Edward J. Larson, *Franklin & Washington,* 192.

When Franklin returned to Philadelphia: Edward J. Larson, *Franklin & Washington,* 175.

Virginia was first to call for the conviction: Edward J. Larson, *Franklin & Washington,* 177.

The dinner was more than social: Edward J. Larson, *Franklin & Washington,* 196.

The stalemate was broken: Edward J. Larson, *Franklin & Washington,* 205.

The Southern colonies would not hear of it: https://www.americanacorner.com/blog/ben-franklin-constitution.

Franklin was an abolitionist: https://www.archives.gov/legeslative/features/franklin (accessed May 1, 2023).

On February 3, 1790: https://www.archives.gov/legeslative/features/franklin (accessed May 1, 2023).

The Petition was entered: https://www.archives.gov/legeslative/features/franklin (accessed May 1, 2023).

Acknowledgments

I have always had a great admiration for both Ben Franklin and Walt Disney. Though these men were born two centuries apart, they shared a keen understanding of who we were as Americans during the times in which they lived. My bold premise, that Franklin and Disney are two of the greatest contributors to our American culture seemed like a good challenge to take up. Their stories are rich and contain parallels beyond what I expected, which I discovered as my research proceeded.

Thank you to my friends, who have read drafts of the book, especially Diane Sanabria, Leominster Historical and Genealogical Librarian, who has always supported my efforts with great enthusiasm. Thank you also to Jane Fischer, Robert Salvatelli and Karin Weaver, who also read early drafts of the manuscript and made helpful comments.

Thank you to my editor Kate M. Victory Hannisian and designer Robin Wrighton. Once again, their expertise and professionalism improved this book, like past efforts, in many significant ways. Tom Campbell of King Printing, as always, added much practical advice, and can always be depended upon to help.

Thank you to Tracy Bernard for turning my handwritten scribblings into a typed manuscript, all while keeping our law office running smoothly. Thank you to my brother and law partner, David Bodanza, for his help, including, along with Robin, finding a title for the book. I am blessed to work with David daily and have his counsel and support.

*The author visits the birthplace of Walt Disney.
The home stands on North Tripp Avenue in Chicago, Illinois.*

About the Author

MARK C. BODANZA is a Leominster resident, accomplished writer, avid historian and successful trial lawyer. He has published thirteen books and numerous newspaper columns, and he has been a guest commentator on radio and television programs nationwide.

Mark has also appeared as a lecturer at schools, libraries and colleges throughout the country. He and his wife raised three children and reside in Leominster, Massachusetts, where Mark serves his community in several civic roles. Mark served as Leominster's city solicitor from 1990 to 1994 and is currently Leominster's Ward 4 city councilor and city council president. He also serves as the chairman of the Leominster Board of Library Trustees.

About the Illustrator

STEVEN LEGER is a Leominster native who spent 23 years in California before returning to his hometown in 2010. Leger attended the Art Institute of Boston and the New England School of Art and Design. He has spent his entire career applying his artistic talents to projects as diverse as architectural models, custom signage, specialty milled products and of course illustrations. Leger has a love of history and enjoys the art of visual storytelling through his intricate work.

Benjamin Franklin
1706-1790

The body of Benjamin Franklin, Printer (like the cover of an old book, its contents torn out and stripped of its lettering and gilding), lies here, food for worms; but the work shall not be lost, for it will (as he believed) appear once more in a new and more elegant edition, revised and corrected by the Author.

Epitaph on Himself
[composed in 1728]